A Handbook for Skill Development : Nursery Management of Horticultural Crops

A Handbook for Skill Development :

Nursery Management of Horticultural Crops

Authors:

Deepa H. Dwivedi
Professor
Department of Horticulture
Babasaheb Bhimrao Ambedkar University,
Rae Bareli Road, Lucknow-226 025 (U.P.) India

Navaldey Bharati
Assistant Professor
Maya College of Agriculture and Technology
Selaqui, Dehradun-248 011
Uttarakhand, India

SSPH

SATISH SERIAL PUBLISHING HOUSE
403, Express Tower, Commercial Complex
Azadpur, Delhi-110033 (India)
Phone : 011-27672852, Fax : 91-11-27672046
e-mail : info@satishserial.com, hkjain1975@yahoo.com
Website : www.satishserial.com

Published by :

SATISH SERIAL PUBLISHING HOUSE
403, Express Tower, Commercial Complex, Azadpur, Delhi-110033 (INDIA)
Phone : 011-27672852 Fax : 91-11-27672046
E-mail : info@satishserial.com, hkjain1975@yahoo.com

ISBN 978-93-88020-15-2

Composed, Designed & Printed in India

Preface

Horticulture is a branch of science which deals with the art and technology of growing fruits, vegetables and flowers, besides other crops, such as medicinal plants, mushrooms, plantation crops, etc. Over the past few decades, it has emerged as the most remunerative sector in Agriculture contributing about 30% to agriculture GDP vide increased production of commodities, export, providing food and nutritional security and generation of employment for rural youth and ladies. India, today, is fast emerging as a global service provider in a plethora of fields, since it is home to the largest population of employable youth. There are tremendous employment opportunities all over the globe in the field of horticulture, especially floriculture and landscape architecture, and there is a big demand of skilled persons.

However, there is a lack of such skilled human resource and even a curricula which may train youth in such skills. The government has recently initiated a scheme for training youth in various skills through the Deen Dayal Upadhyay Kaushal Vikas Yojana and academic institutions have been entrusted the task of development of curriculum for different trades under this scheme for certificate, diploma, advanced diploma and Bachelor degree in Vocational studies. Since literature designed specifically for teaching students through practical based teaching is grossly lacking, hence this book entitled "**A Handbook for Skill Development : NurseryManagement of Horticultural Crops**." has been designed with the specific objective of formulating exercises for the students along with a brief description of the theoretical aspects involved, so that they could gain hands on training and expertise in propagation and management of nursery plants. The manual comprises 27 chapters sectioned into 5 sections and it covers all aspects of media, containers, structures for propagation of horticultural crops, sexual and asexual methods of propagation, Hi-tech nursery raising techniques and finally, how to maintain nursery records and packaging and transportation of nursery plants. Since propagation and nursery management is the basic pillar of horticulture, the manual is useful for all students studying horticulture starting at the Intermediate level, B.Sc. as well as M.Sc. and especially for the B.Voc. students studying any trade in horticulture. This is also useful for the skilled human rersource employed in the Government nurseries, development departments, gardeners, commercial nurserymen, amateur horticulturists, etc.

Authors

About the Authors

Deepa H Dwivedi is a Ph.D in Horticulture from the GB Pant University of Agriculture and Technology, Pantnagar. Having started her career as Assistant Professor/Training Associate at the Sher-e-Kashmir University of Agricultural Science and Technology, Srinagar, Kashmir she worked at the RARS/KVK at Leh, Laddakh. Presently, she is involved in teaching and research for post-graduate and Ph.D courses in Horticulture at the Babasaheb Bhimrao Ambedkar University in Lucknow, where she has also initiated a Bachelor degree course in Vocational Studies in Floriculture and Landscape Gardening under the Skill Development Program of the Government of India.

Navaldey Bharati born in 1987 and permanent resident of Jyotiba Nagar, Distt. Rae Bareli, Uttar Pradesh, completed her under-graduation in Botany and Chemistry from Chhatrapati Shahuji Maharaj University, Kanpur (U.P.) in 2008 and Post-graduation in Agriculture (Horticulture) from Babasaheb Bhimrao Ambedkar University, Lucknow (U.P.) in 2010. She has awarded with Gold Medal in post-graduation in year 2010. She has received her Ph.D. (horticulture) degree from Babasaheb Bhimrao Ambedkar University, Lucknow (U.P.) in 2016. She has also qualified ASRB-NET in year 2010. She worked as Assistant Professor (Guest Faculty) to Bachelor in Vocational Studies (Floriculture & Landscape Gardening) course under the skill development programme run by the Central Government in Department of Applied Plant Sciences at Babasaheb Bhimrao Ambedkar University, Lucknow (U.P.). At Present she is teaching as Assistant Professor in Department of Horticulture at Maya College of Agriculture and Technology, Dehradun, Uttarakhand.

Contents

LAB ACTIVITY

Section A:
GENERAL

LAB ACTIVITY-1

Identification of Tools

1.1 Objective

Identification of garden tools and implements used in Horticulture.

S.No.	Tools & Equipments
i)	**Budding/grafting knife:** It is used for performing/budding, grafting operations.
ii)	**Dibbler:** It is used for making holes in the soil into which seed, seedlings or cuttings may be planted.
iii)	**Garden Fork:** It is used for breaking soil clods, loosening as well as for weeding.
iv)	**Garden Rake:** It is used to remove weeds, leaf debris from the field.

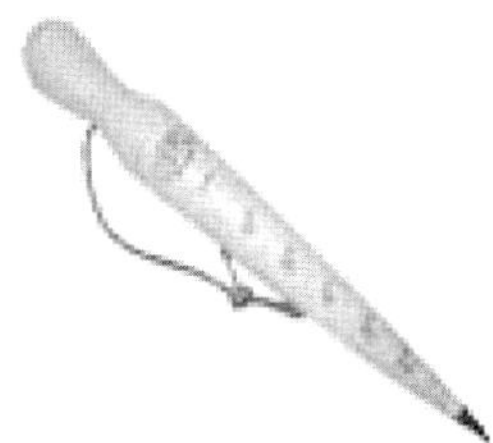

v) **Gloves:** It is used by nurserymen for protection of hands from blisters, calluses, cuts, sun damage and dust.

vi) **Grass Shear:** It is used for clipping grass along the edge of a garden bed, but necessary where prized flowers grow too close to use a mower or string trimmer.

vii) **Hand Axe:** It is used to shape, split and cut wood and to harvest timber.

viii) **Hedge Shear:** It is used for removing whole branches, while hand hedge shears are designed to cut a number of small branches at the same time and to cut woody material up to ½ inch thick.

ix) **Hedge Trimmer**: It is used for trimming (cutting, pruning) hedges or solitary shrubs (bushes).

x) **Khurpi:** It is used for removal of weed and loosening of soil.

xi) **Kneeler:** It is used for protecting knees from sharp stones and prevent clothes from becoming stained.

xii) **Kudali:** It is used for digging pits or digging of soil.

xiii) **Ladder:** It is required for various propagation operations like cutting of scion wood, training of vigorous plants and top working of old and declining plants. (In general, step ladder, straight ladders or hook ladders are used for such operations in the propagation field).

xiv) **Lawn Mower:** It is used for cutting grass to maintain a levelled turf at an even height.

xv) **Lawn Roller:** It is used to prepare soil for planting and pressing grass.

xvi) **Lawn-and-Leaf Rake:** It is used for collecting lightweight material, such as clippings and leaves.

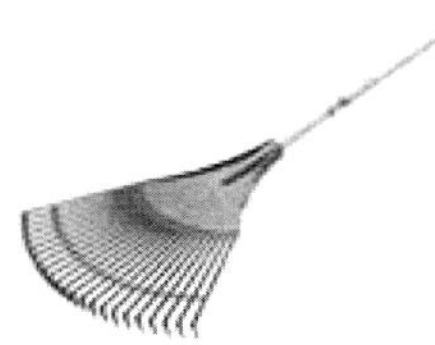

xvii) **Manual Aerator:** It is used for food aeration in lawn facing the problem of thatching of lawn gass. It is foot-powered and easy-to-use.

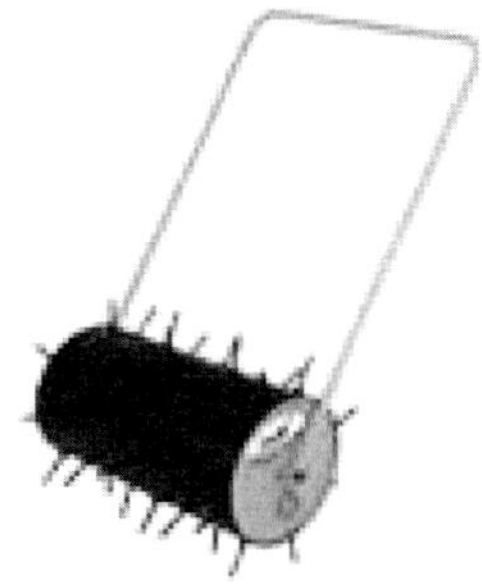

xviii) **Power Tiller:** It is ideal for alleviating compaction in preparation for a new lawn or for mixing in soil amendments, such as lime, fertilizer and compost.

xix) **Pruning Knife**: It is used for cutting small branches or performing various tasks requiring a light cut.

xx) **Pruning Saw:** It is used for woody cutting branches upto three inches in diameter.

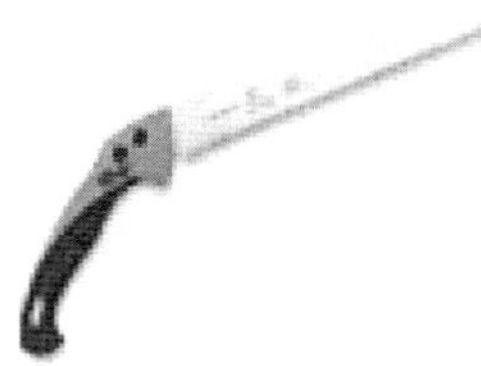

xxi) **Pruning Shears:** It is used to cut thin branches from bushes and small trees during pruning and training operation.

xxii) **Secateurs:** It is used for excising scion, lopping of the rootstocks, removing undesirable sprouts from stocks and training and pruning operations in shrubs.

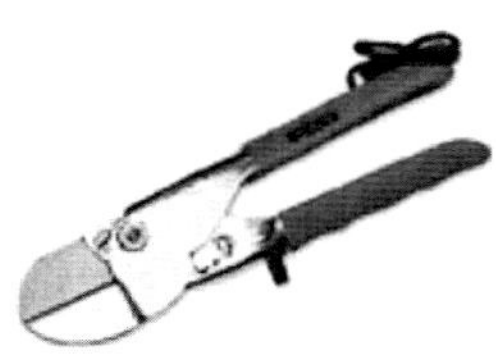

xxiii) **Shovels:** It is used to dig large holes and to transport heavier material, such as wet soil and rocks.

xxiv) **Sickle:** It is used for cutting standing grass, weeds, fodder and harvesting crops.

xxv) **Sod Cutter:** It is for cutting sod into strips.

xxvi) **Spade/Hoe:** It is used for digging pits, making irrigation or drainage channel and for earthing up.

xxvii) **Sprayer:** It is used for dispensing insecticidal, soap or oil solutions.

xxviii) **Spreader:** It is used to distribute seed, fertilizer, and other amendments, such as lime in a row.

xxix) **Thatching Rake:** It is used to remove thatch from lawn without damaging the turf.

xxx) **Tree Pruner**: It is ideal for cutting high branches without climbing a ladder.

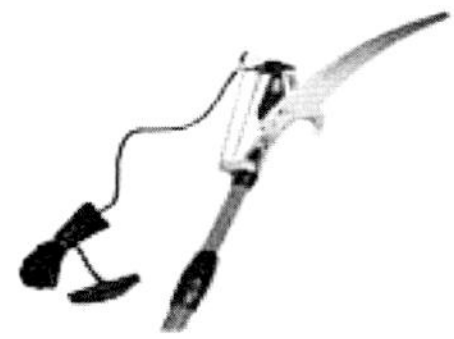

xxxi) **Trowel:** It is used for breaking up earth, digging small holes, mixing in fertilizer or other additives, and transferring plants to pots.

xxxii) **Turf Edger:** It is used to cleanly separate a lawn from a walkway or other paved surface, such as a concrete sidewalk or asphalt path by merely mowing over the border of the lawn and walkway.

xxxiii) **Utility Cart:** It is used to keep gardening tools organized and take them to and from storage.

xxxiv) **Watering can:** It is used for irrigating nursery beds as well as young plants in pots.

xxxv) **Weeder:** It is used for removing weeds from turf.

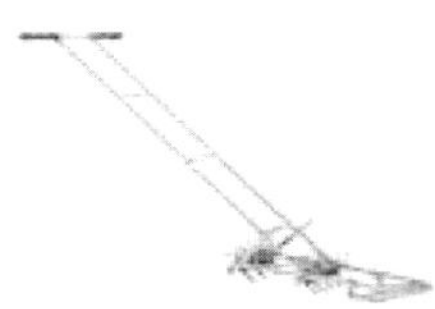

Important Notes

....

....

....

....

....

....

....

....

....

....

Lab Report

1. Identification of garden equipments.
2. List the use of following tools and equipments:

Tools & Equipments	Uses
Spade	
Khurpi	
Secateur	
Kneeler	
Lawn Mower	
Hand Spray	

❑❑❑

LAB ACTIVITY-2

Propagation Media

2.1 Objective

To study media used in plant propagation.

2.2 Introduction

There are several media used by nurserymen for plant propagation through seeds or cuttings. The plant propagating medium must have the following characteristics:

i) It should be firm enough to hold the seeds or cuttings in place during germination or rooting.

ii) It should have the ability to retain and supply sufficient moisture to the seeds and cuttings.

iii) It should have good aeration and drainage capacity.

iv) It should be free from salt concentration.

v) It should be free from weed and harmful pathogens.

2.3 Media

2.3.1 Soil

It is the upper layer of the earth surface which is the reservoir of all plant nutrients and provides anchorage to growing plants. It is composed of air, water, inorganic and organic matter (both living and non-living). An important physical property of soil is its texture (ratio of sand, silt and clay). The ratio determines the ability of soil to permit aeration, drainage and nutrient holding capacity. Sandy soil provides good aeration and drainage but is poor in nutrient and water holding capacity. Clay soil has good water and nutrient retention capacity but is poor in aeration and drainage. A soil mixture of 40 % sand, 40% silt and 20% clay produces a good loam soil having good aeration, drainage and nutrient as well as water holding capacity.

2.3.2 Sand

It is formed as a result of withering of rocks. Its mineral composition depends on the type of rock from which it has been derived. Sand varies in size and shape of its particles (0.05-2.0 mm) Quartz sand comprising silica is suitable for propagation purposes.

2.3.3 Vermiculite

Expanded mica, known as vermiculite, is widely used a medium for seed germination and rooting of cuttings in advanced countries.

Vermiculite is graded into four types:

No. 1 grade: 5-8 mm

No. 2 grade: 2-3 mm (horticulture grade)

No. 3 grade: 1-2 mm

No. 4 grade: 0.75-1.0 mm

Grade 2 is inert, light in weight, being spongy and porous, it has tremendous capacity to retain water and is neutral in reaction, with high cation exchange capacity. However, it is very flaky and sticks to the hand of workers and to the surface of tools when saturated, it holds too much water and it is not durable as sand or perlite, as it can be easily compressed and breaks apart, when handled in wet condition.

2.3.4 Peat

It contains partially decomposed parts of aquatic vegetation or vegetation growing in humid regions. Its composition depends upon the vegetation from which it has originated and has been classified into three different types:

a) Moss peat- It is derived from least decomposition of sphagnum or other mosses. It is highly acidic and has high moisture holding capacity.

b) Reed sedge- It is derived from the decomposition of remains of grasses, reeds, sedges and other swamp plants. pH is between 4.0-7.0 with high moisture holding capacity.

c) Peat humus- It is derived from complete decomposition of hypnum moss or reed sedge peat. It has poor water holding capacity and is the source of weed and pathogens. Thus, it requires pasteurization before using as propagating media.

2.3.5 Perlite

It is grey in colour and prepared by heating glassy volcanic lava in a furnace at about 1200^{0}c. It is almost neutral in reaction with a pH of 7.0-7.5 and has no buffering capacity, cation exchange capacity or mineral nutrients. It can retain water 3-4 times of its weight. It is sterile, free from any pathogen and an ideal rooting medium for cuttings.

2.3.6 Sphagnum Moss

In India, it is found in hills. The dehydrated moss is relatively sterile and light in weight, with a high water holding capacity. It inhibits the growth of molds. and is widely used for keeping live material moist for distant transport. It is also used in air layering of plants.

2.3.7 Leaf Mold

It is prepared by decomposed leaves of various garden plants. Sometimes cow dung, urine or ammonium sulphate is added to enrich it. Leaf mold may contain pathogens, hence, it should be used only after sterilisation. It is used to prepare soil mixture for use as a germination media or for growing plants.

2.3.8 Pumice

Pumice contains silicon oxide and aluminium oxide with varying amount of iron, calcium, magnesium and sodium in oxide form. It increases aeration and drainage in rooting mixtures, if mixed with other propagating media.

2.3.9 Compost

It is prepared by decomposing bulk organic waste under controlled conditions in piles or bins. It is a rich source of mineral nutrients with good water holding capacity. It contains various pathogenic organisms and should be used alone or mixed with soil but only after proper pasteurization.

2.3.10 Shredded bark and saw dust

Shredded bark, saw dust and wood shavings can also be used in mixtures with various propagating media. It is poor in nutrient composition and hence, additional nutrients are added while using as propagating medium. It contains toxic materials like phenols, resins and tannins, etc. and therefore, it should be composted 3-4 months before use.

2.3.11 Cocopeat

It is a by-product of cutting and processing of coconuts for fibre production. It is frequently used as propagating media because of its excellent pore space and fine structure which is ideal for proper growth and development of roots of seedlings. It can be used alone or mixed with other propagating media.

2.4 Criteria for the selection of a propagating media

i) Always select locally available material.

ii) Check the quality of medium before buying it.

iii) Consult with technical expert or a person dealing in nursery business.

iv) Medium must have sufficient porosity and ideal pH (5.5-6.5).

v) Medium should easily mix with other growing medium.

vi) Medium should be free from disease and pest infestation.

vii) Medium should be sterile.

Fig. 2.1 Different media used for plant propagation

Important Notes

....

....

....

....

....

....

....

....

....

....

Lab Report

1. Enlist the various media used for propagation.
2. What points will you keep in mind before selecting a propagating medium?

❑❑❑

LAB ACTIVITY-3

Propagation Structures

3.1 Objective

To study different protected structures used in plant propagation.

3.2 Introduction

Propagation of plants can be performed successfully in open condition but the success is very poor in some plant species. For propagation of plants under unfavourable climatic conditions protected structures are successfully used. Some of theses structures are polyhouse, glasshouse, shade nethouse, hotbed, coldframe and lathhouse.

Some of the protected structures may be equipped with modern microirrigation systems, temperature and humidity controllers, photoperiod regulators, etc.

3.2.1 Polyhouse

It is a greenhouse covered from all sides with polythene film, which is UV-stabilised and 0.10-0.15 mm in thickness. It is useful for successful production of rooted cuttings and crops in severe winter also.

Fig. 3.1 Polyhouse

3.2.2 Glasshouse

A green house covered with glass on all sides is a glasshouse. It is very expensive to install and requires modern techniques for generating and controlling heating and cooling. It is generally equipped with elaborate gadgets for environmental control.

3.2.3 Nethouse

It is installed, where artificial heating is not necessary and cooling is difficult and expensive. Under such conditions, nethouse is an excellent alternative for raising seedlings and cuttings and for other propagation operations. The roof of nethouse may be covered with glass or polythene film, and sides covered with wire net/shade net.

Fig. 3.2 Nethouse

3.2.4 Hotbed

A hotbed is used for germinating seeds, etc. in cold climates. It consists of three parts: the frame, the cover and the heating system. The frame is made of wood, steel, aluminium or concrete. The cover is made of glass or plastic. Artificial provision of heat is provided from the base of the propagating medium by hot air, steam or hot water, which runs in pipes embedded in the soil, or by a soil heating electrical cable. It is mostly used in western countries not in India due to its high cost of installation.

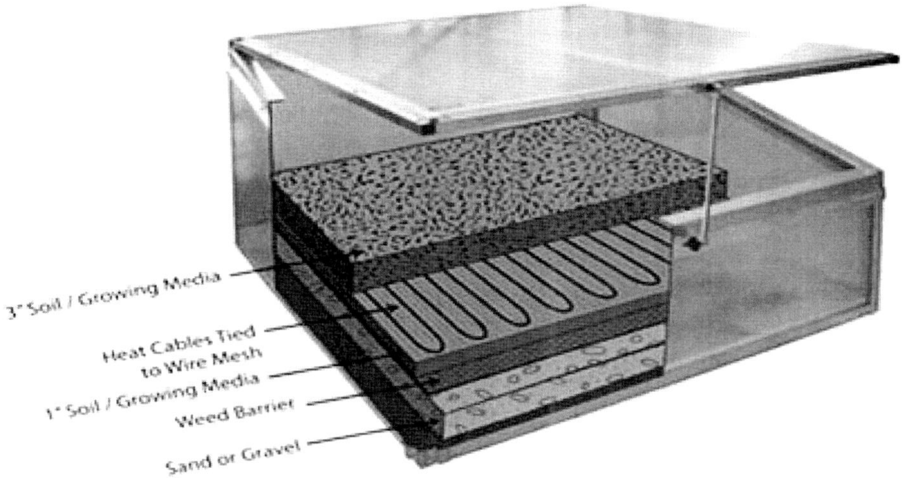

Fig. 3.3 Hotbed

3.2.5 Coldframe

It is an enclosed ground bed, sometimes sunken, with a removable sash. Heat is generated through the trapped sunlight. The coldframe should be located in a sunny place, protected from cold wind. It is inexpensive and used for raising early seedlings from seeds as well as for hardening or conditioning of young seedlings in places, where winter is severe.

Fig. 3.4 Coldframe

3.2.6 Lathhouse or Shadehouse

It is useful for protecting young seedlings or rooted cuttings from the external high temperature and light intensity and hardening them before transplanting in field. Lathhouse acts as an intermediate step between greenhouse, hotbed or coldframe and field planting. Various shading material may be used, thus allowing different intensity of light into the shadehouse.

Fig. 3.5 Lathhouse

3.2.7 Mist Propagating Unit

It is useful for rooting of cuttings which are difficult to root. Mist beds are constructed within the greenhouse. It is set up on propagation beds of 1.2m width. Each bed must be provided with drainage holes for draining excess water. There must be a continuous supply of water for misting. The water should be clean and uncontaminated.

Fig. 3.6 Mist propagating unit

3.3 Advantages of propagating structures

i) Propagating structures make it possible to grow early seedlings of crops.

ii) Accelerate rooting of the difficult to root plants and increase success rate of rooting of cuttings.

iii) In polyhouse with fan and pad cooling system, rooting of cuttings is possible round the year.

iv) Structures like mist propagation unit permit the rooting of soft and succulent material easily rather than older, mature and hardened wood.

v) Plants can be propagated easily in areas with extreme winter and summer season.

vi) Large number of plants can be produced in a short period of time.

vii) Disease, insect, pest and pathogen attacks can be controlled more effectively.

3.4 Limitations of propagating structures

i) High installation cost of the propagation units.

ii) Regular prophylactic measures for incidence of diseases is required.

iii) Require knowledge and skill for operating propagation units.

Important Notes

....

....

....

....

....

....

....

....

....

....

Lab Report

1. Enlist various propagating structures.

Structure	Purpose in propagation

2. Give the advantages and disadvantages of propagating structures.

❐❐❐

LAB ACTIVITY-4

Propagation Methods

1.1 Objective

Study of different methods of propagation in horticultural crops.

1.2 Introduction

Multiplication or perpetuation of plants by sexual or asexual methods is called propagation. The basic objective of plant propagation is to produce offspring from the original plant. Propagation from seed is the sexual method of propagation while propagation by any part of the plant other than seed is called vegetative propagation.

Plant propagation

- Sexual
  - Seed
- Asexual
  - On own Root system
    - **Cutting**
      - -Root cutting
      - -Stem cutting
      - -Leaf cutting
      - -Leaf bud cutting
    - **Layering**
      - -Tip layering
      - -Simple layering
      - -Mound layering
      - -Air layering
      - -Serpentine layering
      - -Trench layering
  - On different root system
    - **Grafting**
      - -Approach grafting
      - -Cleft grafting
      - -Bark grafting
      - -Side grafting
      - -Tongue grafting
      - -Bridge grafting
      - -Top Working
    - **Budding**
      - -Patch budding
      - -T-budding
      - -Chip budding
      - -Ring budding
  - Through special structures
    - -Corm
    - -Bulb
    - -Tuber
    - -Rhizome
    - -Sucker
    - -Runner
    - -Stolon
    - -Tuberous root
  - Micro propagation
    - -Shoot tip culture
    - -Embryo culture
    - - Ovary culture
    - - Ovule culture
    - -Single cell culture
    - -Protoplast culture
    - - Somatic embryogenesis
  - Apomictic seed

1.3 Advantages of Sexual Propagation

i) Only practical method for those plants which cannot be economically raised by other vegetative means.

ii) Seedlings are cheap and can be raised easily as compared to vegetative propagation

iii) New hybrid cultivars are developed by sexual means.

iv) Seed propagation may sometimes result in production of chance seedling of superior trait due to spontaneous mutation.

v) Plants live longer and are hardy as compared to vegetatively propagated plants.

vi) Rootstocks are raised by seeds.

vii) Sexually propagated plants are more resistant to abiotic and biotic stress due to heterozygosity.

1.4 Limitations of Sexual Propagation

i) Seedlings are not true to type due to heterozygous genotype.

ii) Seedlings have long juvenile phase and take more time to come into bearing compared to vegetatively propagated plants.

iii) Plants are vigorous and cultural operations become difficult and expensive.

1.5 Advantages of Asexual (Vegetative) Propagation

i) Plants which do not produce viable seedlings can be propagated easily by vegetative means.

ii) Plants are true to type i.e. they are similar to mother plant.

iii) Vegetative propagation is sometimes easier, rapid and economical than that by seed.

iv) Budding and grafting make the plants adaptable in unfavourable environmental condition.

v) Plants have short juvenile phase and are precocious compared to seedling plants.

vi) Plants are less vigorous and cultural operations are easier.

vii) Injured portion of plants can be removed and vegetatively propagated.

1.6 Limitations of Asexual (Vegetative) Propagation

i) No new variety can be evolved by vegetative propagation.

ii) Vegetative propagation in most of the cases is more expensive than seed propagation.

iii) It requires special knowledge, training and skill of plant propagation.

iv) Vegetatively propagated plants have poor anchorage in soil and can be easily uprooted.

v) They are more prone to pathogenic attack, due to homozygosity than plants propagated through seed.

Important Notes

....

....

....

....

....

....

....

....

....

....

Lab Report

1. List out the major plant propagation methods along with suitable examples.
2. What are the advantage and disadvantage of sexual propagation?
3. What are the advantage and disadvantage of asexual propagation?

❑❑❑

Section B:

SEXUAL PROPAGATION

LAB ACTIVITY-5

Seed Nursery

5.1 Objective

Raising of seed nursery.

5.2 What is a nursery?

Nursery is a place where plants are propagated and grown to usable size for transplanting, sale or experimental study.

The soil of the nursery should be friable, well-drained and fertile to produce vigorous seedlings. It should be well-pulverized before the seed-beds are prepared. The source of irrigation should be near the nursery site. Each seed bed should be raised 15 to 20 cm above the ground level to facilitate drainage. If seedbed is required for raising nursery during the rainy season, it should be raised, while if nursery is prepared during the dry season, then the seedbed should be sunken. Flat bed could be prepared, if the drainage is not a problem.

5.3 Material Required

Spade, *khurpi*, hose can, measuring tape, rope, sand, fungicide, mulch material and farm yard manure.

5.4 Stages of raising nursery

5.4.1 Preparation of seed bed

i) Prepare a seedbed 1.00 to 1.50 m wide and 3.00 m long with the help of spade. Mix well decomposed and fine FYM in the soil at the time of seedbed preparation. Level the bed by breaking the clods and do hoeing with the help of *khurpi*.

ii) Drench the seed bed with chemical fungicide 5g/l to prevent incidence of soilborne diseases.

iii) After 4-5 days of drenching, hoeing should be done again and soil should be mixed properly before sowing of seeds.

5.4.2 Sowing of seed

i) The fungicide treated seeds are sown in lines at a distance of 10 to 15 cm each across the length of the seedbed and at a depth of 2-3 cm depending upon the crop.

ii) Spread a thick layer of sand of about 1.0-1.5 cm over the seed to cover it and prevent the formation of hard crust. The bed may be covered with suitable mulch material to keep the soil moist, if the season is too dry or if there is a scarcity of water. After germination mulch material should be removed.

5.4.3 Aftercare of nursery

i) The seed bed should be watered daily with the help of watering can to prevent water loss and encourage seed germination.

ii) Weed and off type plants should be removed from the bed, as and when they appear.

5.4.4 Transplanting of seedlings

i) Seedlings become ready for transplanting after one or two months. They are dug out and planted in the nursery for hardening. Seedlings of uniform vigour and height should be selected for transplanting for ensuring genetic uniformity. Seedlings should always be transplanted during the evening hours to promote establishment.

ii) At the time of transplanting, dwarf and exceptionally vigorous seedlings should be avoided. The seedlings which have badly crooked roots should also be rejected at this stage.

iii) Before transplanting the main field must be ready for transplanting seedlings. While transplanting seedlings should be planted in line by marking with rope stretched across the field. After every 1.00 m to 1.50 m, a space of about 45-60 cm should be left to facilitate the intercultural operations.

iv) After transplanting a light irrigation is given for proper plant establishment. After one or two weeks gap, filling should be done with new seedlings in the case of mortality.

Important Notes

....

....

....

....

....

....

....

....

....

....

Lab Report

1. Prepare flat nursery beds of size 1.00 x 3.00 m to grow the seedlings of summer annuals.

Name of the summer annual	Quantity of seed	Spacing	Depth of sowing	No. of days taken to germination	Mortality	Days taken transplant

2. Prepare flat or raised nursery beds of size 1.00 x 3.00 m to raise the seedlings of winter annuals.

Name of the winter annual	Quantity of seed	Spacing	Depth of sowing	No. of days taken to germination	Mortality	Days taken transplant

3. Demonstrate seed and soil treatment with different fungicides before sowing to prevent from pathogens.

Fungicides	**Rate of fungicide**	**Soil/seed treatment**	**Duration of treatment**
Captan			
Thiram			
Bavistin			
Formalin			
Fumigation			
Methyl bromide			
Chloropicrin (tear gas)			
Vapam(sodium-N-methyl.dithiocarbomate,dihydrate			

4. Demonstrate the care and maintenance of nursery.

   Number of weeding

   Types of weed

   Frequency of irrigation

   Fertilization

   Fungicide spray, if required

5. Visit to government or private nurseries to learn the advanced nursery raising technology.

❑❑❑

LAB ACTIVITY-6

Seed Viability

6.1 Objective

To study seed viability.

6.2 Introduction

Seed viability refers to the ability of a seed to germinate and produce seedling under favourable conditions. Seed viability can be tested by various methods:

i) Germination test

ii) Tetrazolium chloride test

6.3 Tetrazolium chloride test for seed viability

6.3.1 Principle

A colourless solution of 2,3,5 triphenyl tetrazolium chloride (indicator) reacts with hydrogen released by the reduction process in living cell due to action of enzyme dehydrogenase. It produces a stable and non-diffusible red substance called triphenyl formazan, which helps to distinguish living cells from the colourless dead ones.

6.3.2 Materials Required

i) One per cent solution of tetrazolium chloride at pH 6.5-7.5 is made in water and stored in amber coloured bottle

ii) Conditioning media: blotter, paper towel or beaker

iii) Cutting and piercing device: razor blade, dissecting knives and needles

iv) Staining dishes: watch glass/petridishes

v) Medicine dropper: to remove tetrazolium solution after test

vi) Magnifying device: hand lens

vii) Clearing agent: lactophenol solution.

6.3.3 Procedure

i) 100 seeds which are physically pure should be selected.

ii) Immerse the seeds in distilled water or keep in wet blotter/paper towel for 18 hours to start activity of dehydrogenase enzyme and to facilitate the entry of tetrazoliun solution into the cells.

iii) Remove the testa of dicot seeds and expose the embryo of monocot seeds by bisecting the seed longitudinally after soaking in water.

iv) Then, immerse the seeds completely in 1% tetrazolium solution for 3 hrs at 20° C in dark. Remove the excess solution with dropper and rinse seeds with water and evaluate.

v) After staining small seeds are treated with lactophenol (20 lactic acid: 20 phenol: 40 glycerine: 20 water) to facilitate examination of the seeds, if the pigment within the seed coat prevents clear vision after staining. Then, observations are recorded for number of stained seeds.

6.3.4 Evaluation

The seeds are evaluated with the help of magnifying devices. Each seed is evaluated as viable or dead on the basis of staining pattern in embryo and cotyledons.

Staining of Embryo	
Completely stained	viable
Unstained	non-viable
Plumule or radical unstained	non-viable
Staining of cotyledons	
Complete staining	viable
Unstained	non-viable

6.3.5 Calculation

The results are reported as percentage of viable seeds in relation to total seed tested.

$$\%\ \text{viability} = \frac{\text{Number of seeds stained}}{\text{Total number of seeds}} \times 100$$

Important Notes

....

....

....

....

....

....

....

....

....

....

Lab Report

1. Assess the viability of flower seeds.

	Seed Number						
	1	2	3	4	5	6	7
Embryo							
Complete staining							
No staining							
Radical or plumule stained							
Cotyledons							
Complete staining							
No staining							

Calculation:

Results:

Conclusion:

❑❑❑

LAB ACTIVITY-7

Seed Germination

7.1 Objective

To study germination percentage of seeds.

7.2 Introduction

What is seed?

Mature/ripened ovule from ovary of the flower from which a new plant is formed. It is a unit of sexual propagation.

Germination

Seed germination refers to the resumption in the growth of embryo under favourable environmental conditions. Seed germination test is an index of the capacity of seeds for producing normal healthy seedlings under optimum conditions.

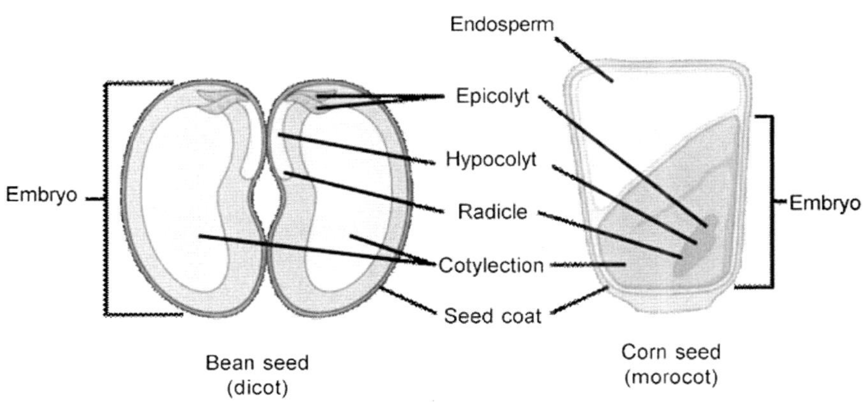

Fig. 7.1 Structure of seed: A. Dicot B. Monocot

7.3 Materials Required

i) Seed of any plant: 100 seeds.

ii) Germinating media: the germinating media must be free from micro-organisms, toxic substances, insects, foreign seeds and should have good water holding capacity and normal pH (6.0-7.0). The media may be sand, filter paper/blotting paper or paper towel.

iii) Water: Distilled and deionised.

iv) Seed germinator: It is a chamber with facilities to manipulate temperature and photoperiod as per need with 100% humidity.

7.4 Covered Petridish Test

Procedure

i) Take four pairs of oven dried petri dishes.

ii) Cut a blotting paper of the same diameter as that of petridish. Place 3-4 layers of blotting paper in each dish. Mix the seed thoroughly.

iii) Count hundred seeds to be tested. Divide the seeds randomly in 4 lots of 25 seeds each. Place seeds in each petridish at uniform distance. Moisten the blotting paper and cover the petridish which is then placed at temperature 20-23^{0}C, depending upon the crop seed.

iv) Keep the blotting paper moist by sprinkling water, as and when required. Do not allow the blotting papers to become dry.

v) Count and remove the sprouted seed on every alternate day. Record the data.

7.5 Paper Towel Method

Procedure

i) Stretch a moist paper towel on a clean table and on other side of the paper towel arrange 50 seeds on its half portion containing 5 rows of 10 seeds each. Leave about 3 cm space on lower and right side of the paper towel.

ii) Cover seeds with remaining half portion of the towel and fold the right and lower portion upward to close both the ends.

iii) Roll the paper towel from the right end, wrap in a wax paper and tie the ends with rubber bands.

iv) Place this paper towel vertically in a seed germinator with open end in upward direction.

7.6 Sand Method

Procedure

i) Immerse sterilized sand in distilled water.

ii) Remove excess water by keeping a handful of this sand in air and place in a tray of 6-9 cm depth.

iii) Count seeds and plant on the levelled sand at proper distance and cover with a layer of dry sand.

iv) Place the tray in seed germinator.

7.7 Evaluation

Critically evaluate each seedling on the day of first count (day on which germination is counted). Count seedlings with all essential normal structures and decayed are removed. Leave the remaining seeds and seedlings as such and evaluate on the day of final count (day upto which the seed should germinate). Record the data as per observation table given in the report.

7.8 Calculation

Express germination as percentage by dividing number of germinated seedlings with the sum of the germinated and ungerminated seeds which is multiplied by 100.

$$\%\,\text{germination} = \frac{\text{Germinated seeds}}{\text{Total number of seeds}} \times 100$$

Important Notes

....

....

....

....

....

....

....

....

....

....

Lab Report

1. Assess the germination percentage of seeds of any five flowering seeds and winter annuals each.

   Crop:

   Variety:

   Seed sample no.

   Date of placing:

   Replications:

   Temperature in °C:

   Germinating media:

   Date of observation:

   Observations Table:

   Variety .... Temperature .... Date ....

Replication	Total no. of seeds	No. of seed germinated (on different days)							Total no. of normal seeds germinated	Total no. of abnormal seeds germinated	Total no. of un-germinated seeds	Germination percentage
		2nd	4th	6th	8th	10th	12th	14th				
1												
2												
3												
4												
5												

Calculation:

Results:

Conclusions:

2. Compare the results of germination by different methods.

LAB ACTIVITY-8

Seed Test Weight

8.1 Objective

Determination of test weight (thousand seeds) of a seed sample.

8.2 Introduction

Test weight is the weight of 1000 seeds in the case of small sized seeds and 100 seeds for bold seeds and is specific for different varieties of a crop.

This test is conducted to determine the boldness and soundness of the seeds. The weight of a given number of seeds of different varieties or kinds varies due to boldness and soundness of the seeds which depends on the soil fertility, variety and other growing conditions. Higher the weight of seeds of a variety per thousand seeds, better is the variety for cultivation.

8.3 Materials Required

Weighing balance and seeds.

8.4 Procedure

i) Prepare a uniform seed sample by mixing seeds thoroughly.

ii) Count three to four lots (replications), each of hundred or thousand seeds for each variety as per the size.

iii) Record the weight of each lot separately, as given in observation table in lab report.

8.5 Result

Test weight = weight in gram/1000 seeds.

8.6 Conclusion

Seed samples having bold seed always record higher weight per thousand seed.

Important Notes

....

....

....

....

....

....

....

....

....

....

Lab Report

1. To determine that samples having bold seed always record higher weight per thousand seed.

   Observation table:

   Crop .... Variety .... Sample No. ....

Date	Variety	Weight (g)				
		Rep. 1	Rep.2	Rep.3	Total	Mean
	A					
	B					
	C					
	D					
	Mean					

   Results:

   Conclusions:

2. Study the difference of thousand seed weight of any ten winter annual seed.

❑❑❑

LAB ACTIVITY-9

Seed Treatment

9.1 Objective

Seed treatment as an aid to germination.

9.2 Introduction

The purpose of giving pre-germination treatment to seed is to stimulate the germination. Seed treatment softens the seed coat or breaks the dormancy, thus reducing the time required for germination. With certain kinds of seeds, pre-germination treatment is essential for good germination, otherwise they may not germinate at all, or the germination may be delayed considerably. For different kinds of seeds, different treatments are required.

The pre-germination treatments adopted to hasten the germination are as follows:

i) Mechanical scarification or removal of seed coat.
ii) Soaking of seed in water.
iii) Treating seed with boiling water.
iv) Treating seed with inorganic acid.
v) Treating seed with chemical stimulants to break dormancy.
vi) Treating seed for specific temperature requirement.
vii) Treating seed for specific light requirement.

9.3 Materials Required

Hot water, sulphuric acid (H_2SO_4) of commercial grade for acid treatment, beakers (250 ml.), petridishes and blotting paper.

9.4 Pre Germination Treatments

9.4.1 Hot Water Treatment

i) Prepare two lots of 25 seeds each. Take two beakers and place each seed lot in each beaker and label it as 1 and 2.

ii) Pour boiling water in 1st beaker 4-10 times the volume of seed and allow it to remain until water has gradually cooled for 12-24 hours. Pour normal water in beaker 2 and keep it for the same period. The optimum soaking time of seeds may vary from species to species.

iii) Remove the seeds from both beakers and place them in petri dishes separately containing moist blotting paper and label it as 1 and 2, respectively.

iv) Seed of both lots must be sown immediately as drying makes treatment ineffective. Keep the blotter moist.

v) Count and remove the germinated seed at every alternate day. Record the data as outlined in lab report.

9.4.2 Acid Treatment

i) Allow the seeds to dry under ambient temperature and make sure the seed surface becomes dry.

ii) Take four beakers label them as 1, 2, 3 and 4 and fill the beakers with different concentration of commercial grade sulphuric acid *i.e.* 5, 10, 20 and 25 per cent, respectively, @ 1200 ml per kg seed.

iii) Count four lots of 25 seeds to be tested. Put each lot of 25 seeds in each beaker labelled as 1,2,3 and 4. Immerse the seeds for required period at 20°-27°C. Lower temperature require longer soaking period.

iv) Remove the seeds from the acid and immediately wash them thoroughly in clean and cool running water for 10-20 minutes to remove all the traces of acid.

v) Spread the seeds in a thin layer for drying unless wet sowing is preferred.

vi) Count the number of germinated seeds treated with different concentration of sulphuric acid and record data in observation table given in lab report.

9.5 Result

$$\%\ \text{germination} = \frac{\text{Number of seeds germinated}}{\text{Total number of dormant seeds}} \times 100$$

Important Notes

....

....

....

....

....

....

....

....

....

....

Lab Report

1. Treat the seeds of Acacia, *Bombax cieba*, Tulip, Sunflower and Gulmohar with hot water and observe number of days required for germination and germination percentage.

Observation table:

Crop .... Variety .... Sample No. ....

Name of the seed plant	Number of seeds treated with hot water	Number of seeds treated with normal water	No. of seeds germinated (days after)						Total	Germination percentage	Remark
			2nd	4th	6th	8th	10th	12th			

Results:

Conclusions:

2. Study the germination of seed using different concentration of sulphuric acid treatment and compare the result.

Crop .... Variety .... Sample No. ....

Sr. No.	Concentration of acid	Number of seeds	No. of seeds germinated (days after)						Total	Germination percentage	Remark
			2nd	4th	6th	8th	10th	12th			

Result:

Conclusions:

❑❑❑

LAB ACTIVITY-10

Seed Treatment

10.1 Objective

Methods of seed sterilization against seedborne diseases.

10.2 Introduction

Most flower seeds carry infectious pathogens either on the surface (seed infestation) or located inside the seeds (seed infection). Examination of dry seed with naked eyes or with hand lens, of 10-30 times magnification, can reveal the presence of seed borne pathogens. Usually fungi produces symptoms like sunken, discoloured or dried area on the seed surface. The seed borne pathogen may be fungi, bacteria, virus and nematodes which become active as soon as the seed is sown in the nursery bed or in the field. This results in decay of seeds and pre or post-emergence damping off. Damping off is very common in vegetable, fruits and flowering annual seedlings. It is very difficult to obtain pathogen free seed particularly in tropical climate of India. Thus, it is important to treat the seed with chemical, physical factors and bio-control agents to prevent occurrence of disease in the nursery plants. Seed sterilization is basically done by:

a) Chemical methods

b) Physical methods

10.3 Chemical Methods

The chemical may be fungicide, antibiotics or nematicide with different formulations including water dispersible powder, dust or slurries to control specific pathogens.

10.3.1 Rotary dresser method

10.3.1.1 Materials Required

Chemical (fungicide or bactericide) and rotary seed dresser for uniform blending of the seeds with fungicide.

10.3.1.2 Procedure

i) Take 250-300 g of seed and put them in the seed dresser.

ii) Add required amount of chemical (fungicide or bactericide) in seed dresser. The amount of chemical will depend on the quantity of seeds to be sown.

iii) Rotate the dresser in the clockwise direction for 10-15 minutes and then, remove the seed. For certain chemicals, small quantity of water is used in dressing and is called **slurry treatment.**

The standard rates of chemical application for both the methods are given below:

S.No.	Name of chemicals	Amount of chemical (g)	Amount of seed (Kg)
Dry dressing			
1.	Agrosan GN (Dust)	250	100
2.	Thiram 75 (Dust)	250	100
3.	Captan 75 (Dust)	250	100
Slurry treatment (per litre of water)			
1.	Captan 75 (WDP)	250	200
2.	Thiram 75 (WDP)	150	200
3.	Bavistin 50 (WDP)	150	200

10.3.2 Osmotic priming

Aqueous solution of polyethylene glycol (PEG) provides an osmotic environment. Immerse the seed in 20 % PEG containing 0.1 % carboxin. Dry in air and store. This treatment reduces seed borne infection.

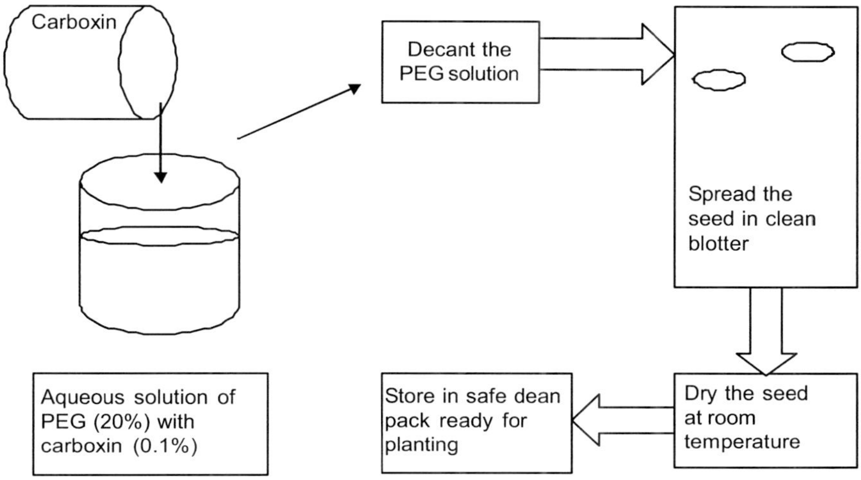

Osmotic Priming

10.3.4 Solid matrix priming

Pre sowing hydration in a solid based medium increases the efficiency of the fungicide in controlling seed borne diseases. Treatment of seed with standard fungicide along with a priming agent effectively controls the seed and soil borne pathogens.

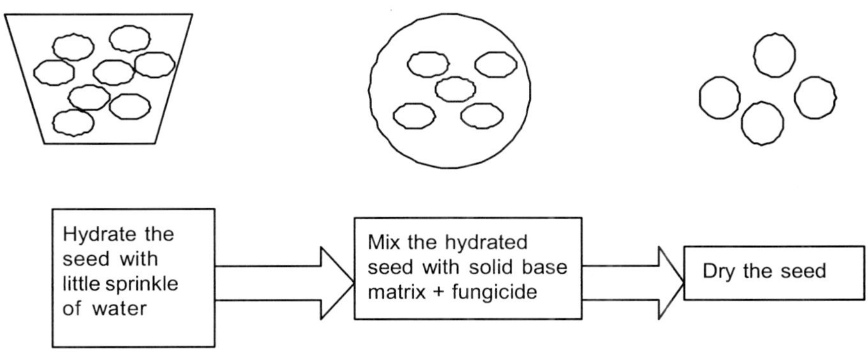

Solid Matrix Priming

10.4 Physical Methods

10.4.1 Seed dip in water

Soaking seeds in plain water at 20^0 C for 40 hours reduces the fungal infection in seed effectively.

10.4.2 Hot water treatment

Dipping the seeds for specific period of time in hot water at a particular temperature safe for the seed embryo and deleterious to the associated pathogen reduces diseases. This method is useful for low volume and high value seed and is effective for internally associated fungi and bacterial pathogen.

10.4.3 Hot air treatment

Exposure of the seed material to hot air stream for a specific period, which is safe for viability of seed and is effective for removal of pathogens present on the seed surface.

10.4.4 Solar treatment

Soaking seed in water for 6 to 8 hours thereby activating the dormant mycelium present in the embryo and subsequently exposing the seed lot to solar heat reduces infection.

10.4.5 Seed seeping

Treating the seed with 20 % commercial salt is called seed seeping.

10.5 Bio-control Agents

Micro-organism used for seed treatment as natural enemy to the pathogens is called bio-control agents. Some bio-control agents are as follows:

Bio-control agent	Pathogen
Fusarium moniliforme	*Aspergillus flavus*
Gilcoladium roseum &	*Alternaria brassicola*
Trichoderma harzianum	

Important Notes

....

....

....

....

....

....

....

....

....

....

Lab Report

1. Treat the seeds of winter and summer annuals with fungicide, physical factors and bio-control agents to find out the percentage of seedling showing disease symptoms.

   Observation table:

   Crop .... Variety ....

Method of seed treatment	Total no. of seeds	Rep. 1	Rep. 2	Rep. 3	Rep. 4	No. of seeds showing disease symptoms	No. of seeds without disease symptoms	Mean
1. Untreated								
2.								
3.								
4.								
5.								
6.								

   Results:

   Conclusions:

2. Compare different methods of seed treatment and state, which one is more effective for control of seed borne diseases?

❑❑❑

LAB ACTIVITY-11

Media Sterilization

11.1 Objective

Methods of soil sterilization against soil borne diseases in nursery.

11.2 Introduction

Soil contains various harmful pathogens (fungi, bacteria, nematodes, termites, etc.) which prevent a healthy seed from growing into an acceptable seedling. Thus, it is essential to eliminate these pathogens from the soil by any of the following methods:

a) Physical methods

b) Chemical methods

c) Biological methods

11.3 Physical Methods

11.3.1 Steam sterilization

The seed pans or boxes or flats containing soil are inserted into sterilization chamber and treated for half an hour with steam or heat under pressure at about 100°C.

11.3.2 Perforated pipes

Perforated pipes connected with a high pressure boiler are passed under the nursery beds to sterilize soil. Beds are covered with canvas and the steam is released under cover to raise the soil temperature up to 100°C.

11.4 Chemical Methods

11.4.1 Formalin

Treat the soil with two percent formalin (formaldehyde) which is mixed thoroughly with the soil and then, covered with tarpaulin or gunny bag for 48 hours so that the fumes may sterilize the soil.

11.4.2 Fungicides

Some fungicides, such as benlate, captan, bavistin, brassicol and blitox are used for soil sterilization. A solution of 1-2 per cent is used to drench the soil to be sterilized.

Following are the chemicals used for soil sterilisation:

S.No.	Name of chemicals	Amount of chemical (g/lit.) or %
1	Captan 75 (WDP)	2-4
2	Thiram 75 (WDP)	2-4
3	Bavistin 50 (WDP)	2-3
4	Dithane M-45	4-5
5	Maneb	6-8
6	Benlate	2
7	Blitox	2-3
8	Formalin	1-2 %

11.5 Biological Methods

Micro-organisms used for soil treatment as natural enemy to soil pathogens are called bio-control agents. These bio-control agents control the pathogen population through antagonistic interaction between them.

Bio-control agent	Pathogen
Fusarium moniliforme	*Aspergillus flavus*
Gliocladium roseum &	*Alternaria brassicola*
Trichoderma harzianum	
Pseudomonas fluorescens F113	*Pythium spp.*
Agrobacterium radiobacter	*Agrobacterium tumefaciens*
Bacillus subtilis AU195	*Aspergillus flavus*
Trichoderma virens	*Rhizoctonia solani*
B. subtilis (BBG100)	*Pythium aphanidermatum*

Important Notes

....

....

....

....

....

....

....

....

....

....

Lab Report

1. Treat the nursery beds with different physical, chemical and biological methods and find out the percentage of seedling without any disease. (seed must be healthy and treated with fungicide)

Observation table:

Methods of soil treatment	Total no. of seeds sown	Rep. 1	Rep. 2	Rep. 3	Rep. 4	No. of seeds showing disease symptoms	No. of seeds without disease symptoms	Mean
1. Untreated								
2.								
3.								
4.								
5.								
6.								

Result:

Conclusion:

2. Compare different methods of soil treatment and report which one is more effective to prevent pathogen attack?

❑❑❑

LAB ACTIVITY-12

Plant Bioregulators in Propagation

12.1 Objective

Studies on the effect of plant bioregulators (PBR) on the development of plants.

12.2 Introduction

Plant hormone is an organic substance produced naturally by the plant or may be applied artificially in very small quantity (μg level). These substances are produced in one part of the plant and translocated to another part and regulate physiological activities of the plant like growth, flowering, etc.

Plant bioregulators may be either growth enhancing substances or retarding substances.

The major kinds of plant bioregulators are:

- Phytohormones or naturally occurring growth substances
- Synthetic hormone like substances
- Synthetic growth retardants

In cultivation of certain crops, sometimes it may be desirable to modify the growth and development of the plants which results in earlier and better quality crop. The earliness or increased yield may be due to reduced vegetative growth or increase in plant size or portion of the plant which is of economic importance. Plant growth is usually modified, when plants are young. The young seedlings respond better to treatment. However, it is not uncommon to modify the growth of the plant even at a later stage.

It should be kept in mind that all hormones are growth regulators but all growth regulators are not hormones.

12.3 Role of growth regulators in seedling growth

S. No.	Purpose	Growth regulator	Suggested rate	Remark
1.	Accelerating seedling growth	i) Gibberellic acid (GA_3)	20-80 ppm	Foliar application 2-3 times
		ii) 2, 4 dichlorophenoxy acetic acid	1-5 ppm	Repeat spray after 7-10 days
2.	Increasing plant height	i) Gibberellic acid (GA_3)	25-100 ppm	2-3 spraying
3.	Increasing compactness and reducing plant height	i) Daminozide	2500-5000ppm	Foliar application or soil drenching
		ii) Chlormequat chloride (Cycocel)	1000-3000 ppm	2-3 spraying or 2-3 soil drenching
		iii) Maleic hydrazide (MH)	100-200 ppm	Foliar spray 2-3 times

12.3.1 Accelerating Seedling Height

12.3.1.1 Materials Required

Chemical balance, beaker, volumetric flask, gibberellic acid, 95% alcohol, clay pots, sprayer and wetting agent.

12.3.1.2 Procedure

i) Take 12 pots and fill them with well decomposed FYM. Sow 4-6 seeds of dog Flower, calendula, phlox or petunia in each pot.

ii) Irrigate the pots, as and when required. When the seedlings are 8-10 cm tall, thin them to 3-4 seedlings per pot.

iii) Divide the pots in four groups, having three pots in each group.

iv) Prepare three concentration of gibberellic acid (50 ppm, 100 ppm and 150 ppm) and spray each group of seedling with one concentration of solution.

v) Keep one set of seedlings as control receiving only distilled water.

vi) Repeat spraying after 7-10 days. If necessary, one more spraying may be given after 7-10 days. Record the observations.

12.3.2 Inducing compactness and retarding seedling height

12.3.2.1 Materials Required

Chemical balance, beaker, volumetric flask, cycocel, 95% alcohol, clay pots, sprayer and wetting agent.

12.3.2.2 Procedure

i) Take 12 pots and fill them with well decomposed FYM. Sow 4-6 seeds of dog Flower, calendula, phlox or petunia in each pot.

ii) Irrigate the pots, as and when required. Maintain 1-2 plants in each pot till the seedlings are 10-12 cm tall.

iii) Divide the pots in four groups, having three pots in each group.

iv) Prepare three concentration of cycocel (1000 ppm, 1500 ppm and 2000 ppm) and spray each group of seedling with one concentration of solutions prepared.

v) Keep one set of seedlings as control receiving only distilled water.

vi) Repeat spraying after 7-10 days. If necessary, one more spraying may be given after 7-10 days. Record the observation in table given in lab report.

12.4 Conclusion

Growth regulators play important role in controlling plant growth. The plant height can be manipulated with the aid of growth regulator, when applied at suitable concentration and stage of growth.

Important Notes

....

....

....

....

....

....

....

....

....

....

Lab Report

1. Use seedlings of varied age group of winter annuals and find out the age group which respond maximum to the chemical treatment.

Concentration growth retardant	Seedling height at start (cm)	Seedling height after (days)				Fresh and dry weight of seedling (g)		Leaf area ratio (LAR)		Remark
		7	14	21	28	start	end	start	end	

2. Use growth retardants on summer and winter flowering annuals.

Concentration growth retardant	Seedling height at start (cm)	Seedling height after (days)				Fresh and dry weight of seedling (g)		Leaf area ratio (LAR)		Remark
		7	14	21	28	start	end	start	end	

3. Use growth retardants on indoor plants and observe their performance.

Concentration growth retardant	Plant height at start (cm)	Plant height after (days)				Fresh and dry weight of plant (g)		Leaf area ratio (LAR)		Remark
		7	14	21	28	start	end	start	end	

❑❑❑

LAB ACTIVITY-13

Plant Nutrition

13.1 Objective

To identify the sources of primary/secondary nutrients and complex fertilizers.

13.2 Introduction

Plants require about 16 essential nutrients for normal growth and development. Some nutrients are needed in large amounts, while others are required only in minute quantities. Regardless of the amount required, a deficiency of any of these nutrients will limit the growth and development of plants.

13.3 Criteria for essentiality of nutrients

- Plant is not able to complete its life-cycle under the deficiency of nutrient(s).
- Any nutrient deficiency in a plant can be overcome by the application of same nutrient and this deficiency can not be overcome by any other nutrient.

13.4 Essential nutrients are :

i) **Macronutrient:** Nutrients required in large quantity. These are basic, primary and secondary.

   a) **Basic nutrients:** carbon, hydrogen, oxygen

   b) **Primary nutrients:** nitrogen, phosphorus, potassium

   c) **Secondary nutrients:** calcium, magnesium, and sulphur

ii) **Micronutrients** are iron, manganese, zinc, boron, copper, molybdenum, and chlorine are required only in minute amounts.

13.4.1 Simple fertilisers

The nutrient percentage of the fertiliser sources are given below and they can be identified on the basis of their physical characteristics:

Name of the fertiliser source	Nutrient percentage	Physical characteristics
Sources of Primary Nutrients		
A. Nitrogen fertilisers		
Quick Release Nitrogen Sources		
1. Ammonium Sulphate	26.0	Colourless crystal like sugar
2. Calcium Ammonium Nitrate	25-26	Dull grey, hygroscopic granule
3. Urea	46	Fine white granules
4. Ammonium Chloride	26	White powder/crystal/pellets
Slow Release Nitrogen Sources		
1. Natural Organics		
2. Ureaform		
3. Urea formaldehyde products		
4. Triazones		
5. IBDU		
6. Sulphur coated urea		
7. Polymer coated nitrogen		
B. Phosphatic fertilisers		
1. Single Super Phosphate	16	Ash coloured granules
2. Double Super Phosphate	32	Ash coloured granules
3. Triple Super Phosphate	48	Ash Coloured Granules
4. Ground Rock Phosphate	30	Dark grey powder
C. Potassium fertilisers		
1. Muriate of Potash	60	Crystalline, white or light grey or pinkish hygroscopic in nature
2. Sulphate of Potash	40	Crystalline white
Sources of Secondary Nutrients		
1. Calcium carbonate (agricultural limestone)	32 (Ca)	
2. Magnesium/Calcium carbonate	22 (Ca), 12 (Mg)	
3. Gypsum	22 (Ca), 19 (S)	Grey powder non-hygroscopic

4. Calcium nitrate	19 (Ca)	
5. Epsom salt (magnesium sulphate)	10 (Mg)	Light pink crystalline salt
6. Ammonium sulphate	24 (S)	Colourless crystals like sugar
7. Ferrous sulphate	19 (S)	Light to dark green big crystals
8. Potassium sulphate	18 (S)	Crystalline white
9. Zinc sulphate	21.6 (Zn)	Grey/yellow, brown, crystalline salt
10. Copper sulphate	25.0 (Cu)	Bluish crystal
11. Elemental sulphur	90 (S)	Earthen grey coloured, pulses like pellets

13.4.2 Complex Fertilisers

1. Monoammonium phosphate	11 (N) + 48 (P)	Grey, Granular, non-hygroscopic
2. Diammonium phosphate	18 (N) + 46 (P)	Dark brown, granular non hygroscopic
3. Urea ammonium phosphate	28 (N) + 28 (P)	Grey, Granular, non-hygroscopic
4. NPK fertilisers	10 (N) + 26 (P) + 26 (K)	Grey, Granular, non-hygroscopic

Important Notes

....

....

....

....

....

....

....

....

....

....

Lab Report

1. To identify different nitrogen sources of fertilisers on the basis of their physical characteristics.

Identifying features	Name of the fertilizer	Nutrient percentage
1.		
2.		
3		
4.		

2. Identify and compare quick release and slow release nitrogen fertilisers.

Identifying features	Name of the fertilizer	Nutrient percentage
1. Quick Release		
2. Slow Release		

3. Identify various primary and secondary sources of nutrients.

Identifying features	**Name of the fertilizer**	**Nutrient percentage**
1. Primary Sources		
2. Secondary Sources		

❑❑❑

LAB ACTIVITY-14

Seed Purity

14.1 Objective

Study on the physical purity analysis of seeds.

14.2 Introduction

It is very difficult to obtain seed sample of crop which are hundred per cent pure. Seeds of other crop and varieties, weed seeds and inert materials are invariably present in seed samples. Purity test is necessary to determine the proportion of foreign material or impurities present in seed samples. Thus, the study helps in determining the seed standards for foundation and certified seeds. Seed samples showing high percentage of purity indicate uniform plant population and will require less rouging. There are two methods for determining physical purity of seeds: (1) By number, (2) By weight.

14.2.1 Purity analysis by number

14.2.1.1 Materials Required

Physical purity work board, forceps, cup and hand lens.

14.2.1.2 Procedure

i) Draw the samples of the seeds. Mix the seeds thoroughly and weigh 3-4 samples each of 25-50 g seeds. The size of sample will depend upon the size of individual seed.

ii) Spread the seed uniformly over the physical purity work board.

iii) Separate the seeds from impurities (weed seeds, seeds of other varieties, etc.) with the help of forceps.

iv) If required, use magnifying lens for proper and clear identification of seeds.

v) Separate the seeds into four groups as given in the observation table. This way the entire sample should be worked out.

vi) Separate the impurities from seeds on the basis of visual observation of the following category of seeds and record the data in observation table given in lab report.

Other crop seed: seed of any other crop excluding the crop under consideration.

Total weed seed: seed of any plant which is not yet domesticated.

Objectionable weed seed: these are the defined weed associated with particular crop.

Inert matter: material other than any type of seeds.

14.2.1.3 Result

The result of the purity analysis is reported by number of impurities present in the prescribed quantity (g) of the submitted sample.

$$\text{Number of objectionable seed/kg} = \frac{\text{Number of objectionable seed found}}{\text{Weight of sample}} \times 100$$

14.2.1.4 Conclusion

Seed sample after removal of weed seed and other crop seed, gives the ratio between the pure seed and the impurities.

14.2.2 Purity analysis by weight

14.2.2.1 Material Required

Physical/Precision balance, purity work board, spatula, forceps, cups, seed sample.

14.2.2.2 Procedure

i) Prepare the working sample of desired weight and distribute evenly over the physical purity work board. Remove pure seed, other seed and inert matter with the help of spatula and forceps and kept in different cups.

ii) Weigh multiple seed unit (one fertile floret is attached with sterile or fertile floret) of grasses separately without breaking the attachment and report in percentage.

iii) Multiple seed unit, seed without seed coat and insect damage seeds are considered as inert matter. Examine the insect damaged seed thoroughly and when the extent of damage is more than half of the seed, then the seed are considered as inert matter.

iv) Seed blower is used to remove the light weight inert matter from the seeds of grasses or vice-versa.

v) Weigh all the fractions of seed samples at the end of the physical purity analysis and record the data in table given in lab report.

14.2.2.3 Calculation

Physical purity analysis is based on the sum of the weight of different components and not on the original weight of the working sample.

$$\text{Purity (\%)} = \frac{\text{Weight of pure seed (g)}}{\text{Pure seed (g)} + \text{other seed (g)} + \text{inert matter (g)}} \times 100$$

14.2.2.4 Results

The result of the purity analysis is presented using one decimal place. Component less than 0.05% is reported as trace.

14.2.2.5 Conclusion

Seed sample after removal of weed seed and other crop seed, gives the ratio between the pure seed and the impurities.

Important Notes

....

....

....

....

....

....

....

....

....

....

Lab Report

1. Find out the purity percentage on the basis of number and the name of crop and weed seeds present in dog flower, petunia, pansy, phlox, marigold, salvia and acroclinum

   Observation table:

   Crop .... Variety .... Sample No. ....

Sr. No.	Replication 1		Replication 2		Replication 3		Weight of sample (g)	
	Number	Name	Number	Name	Number	Name		
1. Pure seed								
2. Other crop seeds								
3. Weed seeds								
4. Objectionable weed seeds								
5. Inert material								
Total								

   Results:

   Conclusions:

2. Find out the purity percentage on the basis of weight and the name of crop and weed seeds present in dog flower, petunia, pansy, phlox, marigold, salvia and acroclinum

Observation table:

Crop .... Variety .... Sample No. ....

Component	Weight (g)			Remark
	Replication 1	Replication 2	Replication 3	
Pure seed				
Other seed				
Inert matter				
Total				
Physical purity (%)				

Calculation:

Results:

Conclusions:

❑❑❑

LAB ACTIVITY-15

Propagation: Polyembryony

15.1 Objective

To identify polyembryony in seeds.

15.2 Introduction

When two or more embryos are present in a seed, the phenomenon is called polyembryony. In fruits like citrus and mango polyembryony is a common phenomenon. Polyembryonic seeds generally contain two kinds of embryos, viz. sexual and asexual (vegetative). The sexual embryos are the result of gametic fusion while the asexual embryo develop from the vegetative parts of the mother cell. The phenomenon by which asexual embryo develops is known as apomixes. The seedlings developing from asexual embryo are known as apomicts. The apomictic seedlings are uniform and as good as plants raised by budding, grafting or cutting. The asexual embryo may develop by any one of the following manner:

i) **Recurrent apomixes:** Embryo develops from diploid egg mother cell without undergoing meiotic division e.g. *Rubus sp.* (Raspberry), *Malus hupehensis,* etc.

ii) **Non-recurrent apomixes:** Embryo develops from any haploid cell other than egg of the female gametophyte e.g. *Solanum nigrum, Nicotiana tabacum,* etc.

iii) **Adventitious embryo (nucellar embryony):** when embryo develop from the cell lying outside the female gametophyte from the nucellar tissue e.g. Mango cvs. Olour, Goa, species of citrus except *Citrus medica* (citron), *Citrus grandis* (Pummelo or Shaddock) and *Citrus latifolia, etc.*

iv) **Vegetative apomixes:** When embryo develops from the any vegetative tissue or cell (buds or bulbils) other than female gametophyte e.g. *Poa bulbosa* and some *Allium,* Agave and grass species.

The number of asexual embryos within a seed varies from 2-20. The asexual embryos are usually less vigorous than sexual embryos.

15.3 Materials Required

Watch glass, needle, forcep, beaker, hand lens, vernier callipers, dissecting microscope and lime seed.

15.4 Procedure

i) Take 25 freshly extracted citrus seeds. (In case of previously extracted seeds, soak them in beaker containing plain water for 4-6 hrs.)

ii) Hold the seed by finger and remove the seed coat and testa with the help of forcep and finger. Open the seed in two with the help of needle. Nuceller embryos can be distinguished from the zygotic embryo by their lateral position in the embryo sac, irregular shape, and lack of suspensor.

iii) Separate the two cotyledons. Take out asexual and sexual embryo with the help of needle. Use a hand lens for separating the large and small embryos. The zygotic seedlings are frequently smaller than nucellar seedlings.

iv) Measure the size of large and small embryos with the help of vernier callipers. Record the observation. Dissecting microscope may be used for measuring the size of embryos and record the data in observation table of lab report.

Important Notes

....

....

....

....

....

....

....

....

....

....

Lab Report

1. Study and compare the polyembryony in *kagzi* lemon, Nagpur Orange and Rose apple.

No. of seeds examined	No. of embryos		Size of embryos (mm)		No. of embryo situated laterally in embryo sac	Average no. of embryo	Average size (mm)		Percentage of poly-embryony
	Large	Small	Large	Small			Large	Small	

2. Sow the seeds of lime, lemons, sweet and sour oranges and find out the number of seedlings sprouted and sort out vigorous and less vigorous seedlings.

No. of seeds examined	No. of seedlings sprouted	No. of vigorous seedlings	Size of vigorous seedlings	No. of non vigorous seedlings	Size of non vigorous seedlings	Percentage of polyembryony

❑❑❑

Section C:
ASEXUAL PROPAGATION

LAB ACTIVITY-16

Propagation: Cuttings

16.1 Objective

To study propagation through cuttings.

16.2 Introduction

A cutting is any part of the plant which when put into a suitable propagating medium becomes an individual plant on its own root and is genetically similar to mother plant. Multiplication of plants by cuttings include stem, root and leaf cuttings. Raising plants through cuttings is a simple quick and cheap method of plant propagation. Most ornamental plants are raised by stem cutting, while some plants are also propagated by leaf or root cuttings.

16.3 Principle

Regeneration of plant part (cutting) into an entire plant structure basically depends on the principle of **Totipotency** (capacity of an individual cell to reconstitute all plant parts). Totipotency involves two phenomenons:

a) **Dedifferentiation**: When differentiated living cells that have lost the capacity to divide, can regain the capacity of division under certain conditions.

b) **Redifferentiation**: Such meristems/tissues are able to divide and produce cells that once again lose the capacity to divide but mature to perform specific functions.

16.4 Materials Required

Secateur, water, rooting media, rooting hormone, pot, *Khurpi*, etc.

16.5 Types and Methods of Cutting

16.5.1 Stem cutting

Stem cutting is a piece of stem detached from the main shoot of a plant or any side shoot growing from the same plant or stem and planted in a suitable media to develop into a new individual plant. Stem cuttings are of four types, namely hardwood cuttings, soft wood cutting, semi hardwood cuttings and herbaceous cutting.

16.5.1.1 Hardwood cuttings

i) Hardwood cuttings are prepared during dormant season usually from 1 year old wood of mature shoots of previous season's growth. Select only healthy shoots and avoid the weak fast growing shoots having long internodes.

ii) The length of the cutting varies between 10 to 45 cm in length and 0.5-2.5 cm diameter. The cuttings of 25-30 cm length with pencil thickness should be preferred.

iii) Give a straight cut at base of the shoot below the node while a slant cut 1 to 2 cm above the node at the top of the cutting to identify the polarity of the shoot and also to prevent water from accumulating on the tip of the cutting protecting it from fungal infection.

iv) Cuttings should be immersed in water to prevent water loss and should be planted, when the climate is moist and humid.

v) During planting 2/3 portion of the cutting should be embedded in the rooting media keeping 1/3 portion above the surface. Before planting, cuttings may be treated with rooting hormone to enhance root formation in the cuttings. Plants like *Ficus, Rose, Bougainvillea, Gliricida, Erythrina, etc.* are propagated by hard wood cutting.

16.5.1.2 Semi hardwood cuttings

i) Semi hardwood cuttings are prepared from partially mature slightly woody shoot. These are succulent and tender in nature and are usually prepared from growing wood of current season growth.

ii) The length of cutting varies from 7 to 15 cm. Treatment of the cuttings with rooting hormones (IBA, NAA, etc.) before planting gives better root formation.

iii) One quarter of the length of cutting should be below the soil. Plants like jasmine and hydrangeas are propagated by semi hardwood cutting.

16.5.1.3 Soft wood cutting

i) Soft wood cutting are prepared from soft succulent and non lignified shoots which have not become hard or woody.

ii) Size of cutting should be 5-7 cm. Some leaves should be retained with this type of cutting to continue photosynthetic activity. Before planting, treatment with auxin is beneficial to enhance rooting in cuttings. Ornamental plants like *Duranta, Iresine,* etc. are propagated by softwood cuttings.

16.5.1.4 Herbaceous cutting

i) In some plant species, terminal leafy portion of the stem is used for preparing herbaceous cuttings. Herbaceous cutting rooted under the same condition as the soft wood cutting but require more relative humidity than soft wood cutting.

ii) About 8.0 to 12.0 cm of a herbaceous tip is cut and basal leaves are removed leaving two terminal leaves. Herbaceous cuttings of some plant exude a sticky sap as in geranium, cactus, etc. that interfere with the root initiation process. In such cases, cutting should be allowed to dry for few hours before planting. Some flowering plants like Dahlia, Carnation, Chrysanthemum, Coleus, Delphinium, Petunia and Gerbera are propagated successfully through herbaceous cutting.

Fig. 16.1 Herbaceous Cutting

16.5.2 Root cutting

Root or a part of root has the capacity to regenerate a new shoot system or into a new plant under favourable conditions, in some plant species.

i) Root which is 1 cm thick and 10 to 15 cm long are cut into pieces. The best time for taking root cutting is late winter or early spring when the roots are well-supplied with stored food material but before new growth starts. It is important to maintain the correct polarity of root cutting to avoid planting upside down.

ii) The proximal end of the cutting should have straight cut and distal end should have slant cut. Insert the cutting vertically so that the top (proximal end) is above desired level. However, in some cases, horizontal planting give a satisfactory results as in Pelargonium, Achillea, Anemone, Gypsophila, Gaillardia, Phlox,

iii) After planting irrigate the cutting immediately. Plants like Salvia, Aralia, Campsis, Clerodendron, Lagerstroemia, Wisteria, Yucca, etc. can be easily propagated by root cuttings.

16.5.3 Leaf cutting

Leaf, leaf blade or leaf sections are used for multiplication of plants. Leaf cutting should be made from fully expanded recently mature leaves and old leaves may be avoided. Leafy cuttings require environmental conditions similar to herbaceous cuttings for high success relative humidity should be a little high like *Bryophyllum, Kalanchoe, Sedum, Peperomia, Saintpaulia, Viburnum* and *Begonia rex.*

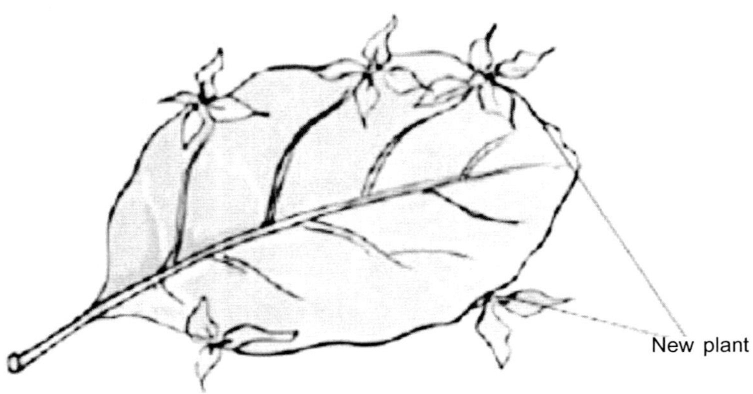

Fig: 16.2 Leaf cutting

Important Notes

....

....

....

....

....

....

....

....

....

....

Lab Report

1. Propagate ornamental shrubs through different methods of cutting.

Name/Type of the plant	Type of Cutting	Number of cuttings planted	Date of planting of cuttings	Days to sprouting	Number of cuttings rooted	Percentage of rooted cuttings	Average root length	Rate of survival after transplanting in field

Result:

Precautions:

2. Visit to various nurseries to learn the propagation through cuttings of other ornamental plants.

❑❑❑

LAB ACTIVITY-17

Propagation: Layering

17.1 Objective

To study propagation through layering.

17.2 Introduction

The method of inducing root in a stem which is still attached to the plant, and then detaching it for transplanting after the root is formed is known as layering or layerage. Mostly shrubs, creepers and trees are raised by this method.

17.3 Principle

Manipulations in shoot or stem like notching, girdling, wounding etc causes interruption in the downward translocation of the organic material like carbohydrate, auxin and other root promoting factors. This material gets accumulated near the upper region of the girdled stem which ultimately induces rooting in that region due to totipotency in the cells. Layering is done during the active season, when the mother plants are growing during July and September.

17.4 Materials Required

Grafting knife, secateur, rooting media, rooting hormone (IBA), pot, transparent polythene strip, tying material, etc.

17.5 Types and Methods of Layering

17.5.1 Simple layering

This method requires just bending down a flexible branch to the ground and covering a portion of it with 6 to 12 cm deep soil, leaving 10 to 30 centimetre of the tip above the ground. The branch is held in position with the help of stone piece or hooks or pegs. The aim is to hinder sap flow at the bend to accelerate root formation. Root formation takes place in about 3 weeks to 3 months depending on the species.

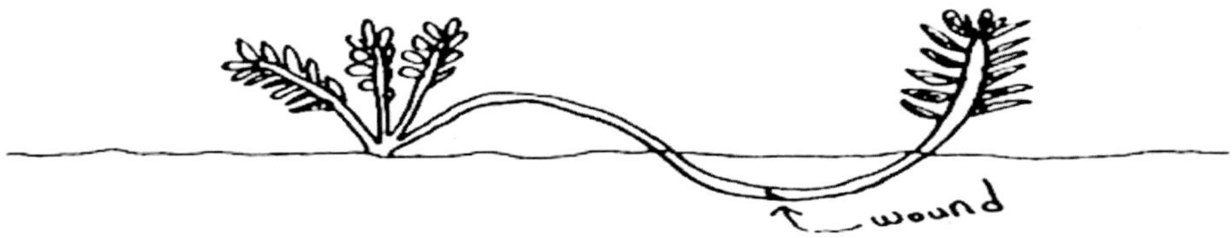

Fig. 17.1 Simple Layering

17.5.2 Mound or stool layering

Short stemmed and stiff branched shrubs are raised by this method. Such plants are encouraged to produce many shoots from the ground level by cutting back the main stem of the previous season. All the branches are wounded near the ground and earthing up (10 to 20 cm height) is done to form a mound around the branches.

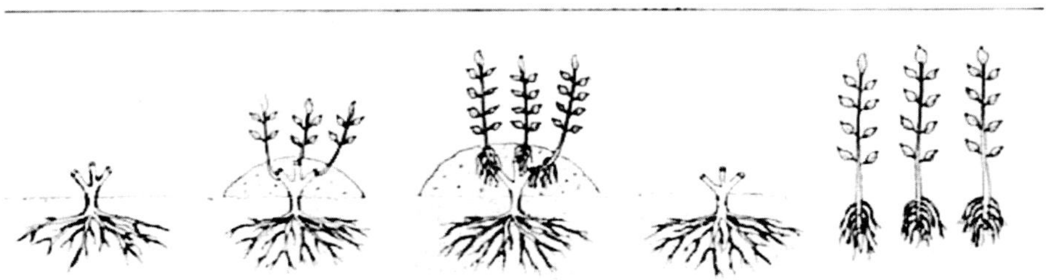

Fig. 17.2 Mound Layering

17.5.3 Compound or serpentine layering

In this method, the stem is covered at several points with soil alternating with other points which are not covered. A similar slit as in simple layering is made at each node covered. Long running roots of vines which are used in this method give rise to several plants.

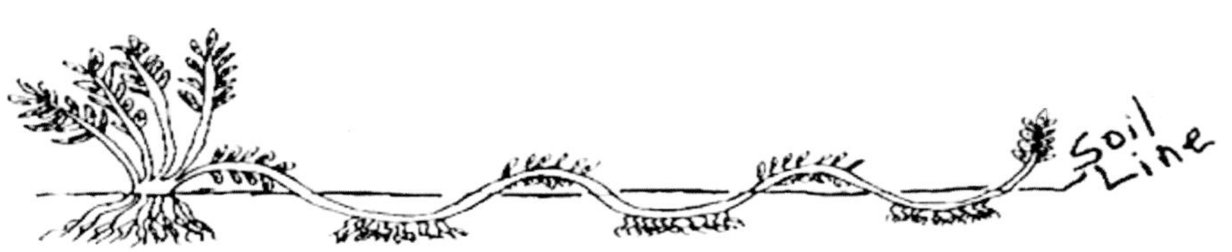

Fig. 17.3 Serpentine Layering

17.5.4 Tip layering

This is similar to simple layering the only difference being that while in simple layering the tip must remain above the ground, in this method the tip is buried in the ground.

17.5.5 Air layering

Branches of plants which cannot be bent to ground level for layering are propagated by air layering. The terminal portion is generally air layered. The ripened branch is slit or notched below a node at the desired height as in the case of simple layering. The part of the wounded stem as well as 5 cm on either side of the wound, is covered with damp sphagnum moss, which is covered over by polythene and securely tied at both ends to prevent moss from drying up. Many of the shrubs and creepers are propagated by air layering.

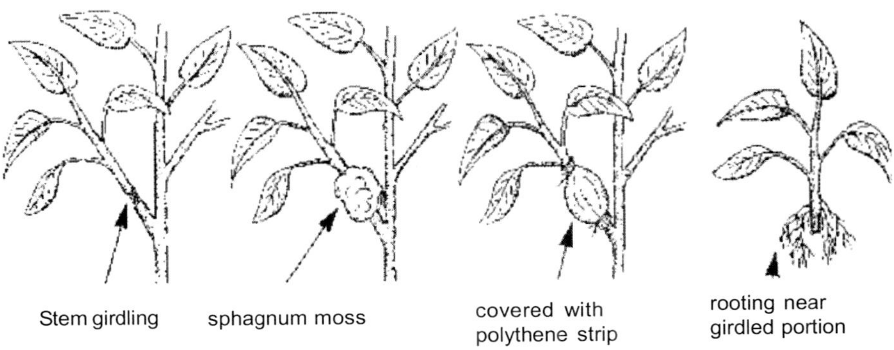

Fig. 17.4 Air Layering

Important Notes

....

....

....

....

....

....

....

....

....

....

Lab Report

1. Propagate ornamental plants through different methods of layering.

Name/Type of the plant	Method of layering adopted	Number of shoot layered	Date of layering	Days to rooting in layers	Number of layers rooted	Percent age of rooted layers	Average root length	Percentage of success after trans-planting in field

Result:

Precautions:

2. Visit to various nurseries to learn the propagation through layering of different ornamental plants.

❑❑❑

LAB ACTIVITY-18

Mother Plant Selection

18.1 Objective

To study selection of mother plant and bud wood.

18.2 Introduction

In propagation of horticultural plants by any vegetative methods, such as cuttings, buddings and graftings due attention should be given to the selection of mother plants and bud wood. Use of budwood or any other propagation material from high yielding, true to type, disease free trees will ensure uniform behaviour of trees. If possible, propagation material from a single parent source should be used.

Bud wood used for budding purpose, which is certified for the above characters by a registered certifying agency is referred as certified bud.

18.3 Procedure

By adopting the criteria given below, clean scion from healthy, productive plants can be obtained.

A. Consideration for selection of mother block

i) Location of the orchard

ii) Location of trees in the orchard

iii) Details about scion

iv) History of the scion

v) History of the orchard

vi) Soil climate and topography

Selection Process

i) Eliminate non-uniform trees

ii) Eliminate diseased trees

B. Criteria for selection of individual trees for mother plant

i) Healthy and vigorous tree

ii) True to type

iii) External characters of fruit

iv) Heavy and regular bearing

v) Freedom from disease

vi) Sufficient availability of bud wood

vii) Study of records for yield and quality

viii) Elimination of unproductive and irregular bearing plants

ix) Study of records for yield, fruit maturity and uniform size of fruit

C. Criteria for selection of bud wood

i) Plumpness of wood

ii) Freedom from thorns

iii) Avoid flower bud (Leaf buds are sharp and pointed)

iv) Branch from which bud is taken, should be round and of lead pencil thickness

Important Notes

....

....

....

....

....

....

....

....

....

....

Lab Report

1. With the help of flow sheet, describe selection of mother plant from an orchard.
2. With the help of flow sheet, select bud wood of rose.

LAB ACTIVITY-19

Propagation: Grafting

19.1 Objective

To study propagation through grafting.

19.2 Introduction

The operation of inserting a part of stem of one plant in another in such a manner that a union takes place between the two parts and they grow together as one plant is called grafting. The part of the plant on which the grafting is done and which provide root system is known as root stock and the upper part, which is united with the stock and is obtained from a superior cultivar is called scion.

19.3 Principle

Establishment of direct contact between cambial region of the stock and scion cause production and interlocking of parenchymatous cells results in production of new cambial cells and formation of new vascular tissues.

19.4 Materials Required

Grafting knife, secateurs, tying material (polythene tape).

19.5 Types and Methods of Grafting

19.5.1 Approach / Inarch grafting

i) Raise the stock plant prepared from cuttings or seed in nursery pot.

ii) Select disease free mother plant to collect scion. Stock and scion should be of same thickness.

iii) Place the stock near the scion plant.

iv) Remove the bark by grafting knife through one-third of the stem in both stock and scion to a length of about 5-7 cm.

v) The cut surface are placed as closely as possible and tied properly with polythene tape. The cuts should be smooth and nearly as flat as possible so that their cambial layers come in close contact with each other.

vi) After 4-6 weeks, when stock and scion are united well, a grafting polytube may be placed over the scion upto graftage portion to prevent water loss and create a stable microclimate. The scion is cut below the union and stock is above the union to produce a new graftage plant.

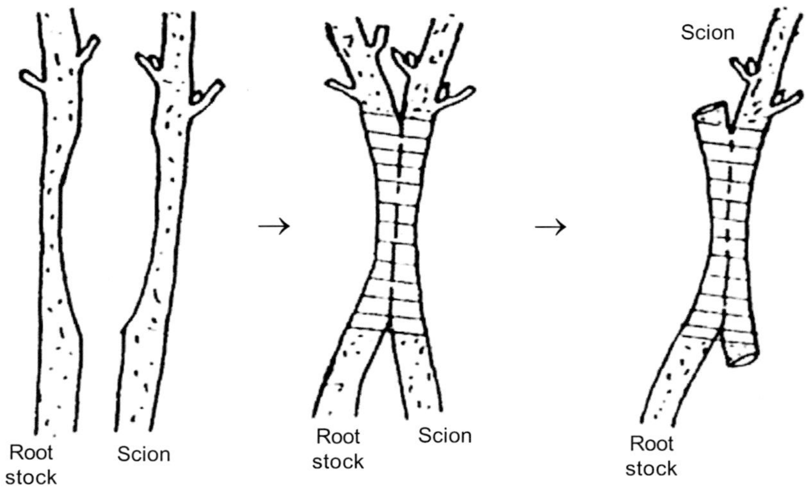

Fig. 19.1 Approach Grafting

19.5.2 Side grafting

i) Raise the root stock plant prepared from cuttings or seed in nursery.

ii) Select disease free mother plant to collect scion from the terminal shoot of 10-15 cm length. Terminal shoots which are plump and swollen and are about to sprout should be selected. Defoliate the scion a week before detaching from the mother plant to prevent water loss and to invigorate the bud. Stock and scion should be of same thickness.

iii) A single oblique cut is made with the help of grafting knife on one side of the stock. A slanting cut of 5-7 cm long is made into the scion wood having 5-6 buds and a similar second slant cut is made on the opposite side of the first cut of scion.

iv) The cut end of the scion is placed on the stock so that the cambium layer of both match. Tightly wrap the graftage with polythene tape.

v) After 4-6 weeks, when union is complete, the rootstock is cut back above the union.

19.5.3 Veneer grafting

i) It is the modified form of side grafting to eliminate the drawbacks of side grafting. In this method, one year old rootstock of 1.0-1.5 cm is selected for grafting.

ii) The rootstock is prepared by making a slant cut of 5 cm long and an oblique cut is made at the base of the first cut so that a piece of wood along with bark is removed.

iii) The base of the scion wood is then fitted into the rootstock in such a manner that the cut surface including the cambium layer of scion and rootstock face each other.

iv) Tightly wrap the graftage with polythene tape. After 4-6 weeks, when union is complete, the rootstock is cut back above the union.

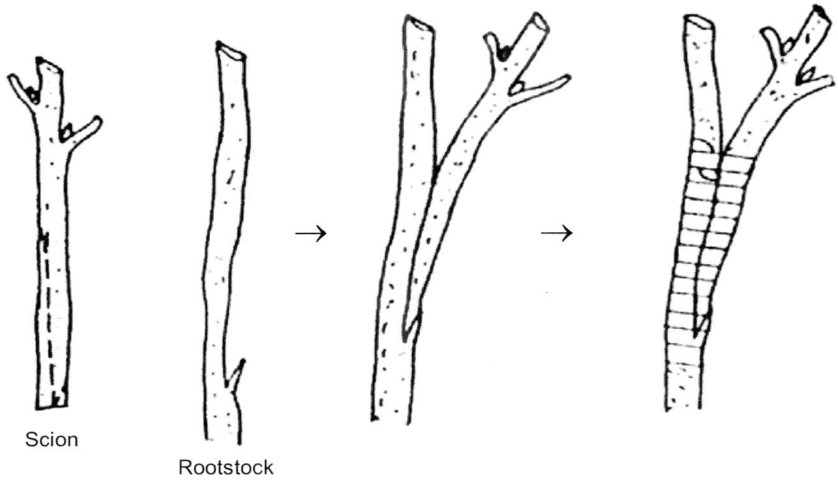

Fig. 19.2 Veener Grafting

19.5.4 Splice or whip grafting

i) Raise the stock plant prepared from cuttings or seed in nursery.

ii) Select disease free mother plant to collect scion of 10-15 cm length from the terminal shoot that is plump and swollen and is about to sprout. Defoliate the scion a week before detaching from the mother plant to prevent water loss and to invigorate the axillary buds. Stock and scion should be of same thickness.

iii) A long slant cut is given at the base of the scion wood and a similar cut is made at the top of the stock with the help of grafting knife.

iv) Tie both stock and scion with the polythene tape tightly.

v) After 4-6 weeks, when union is complete, the rootstock is cut back above the union.

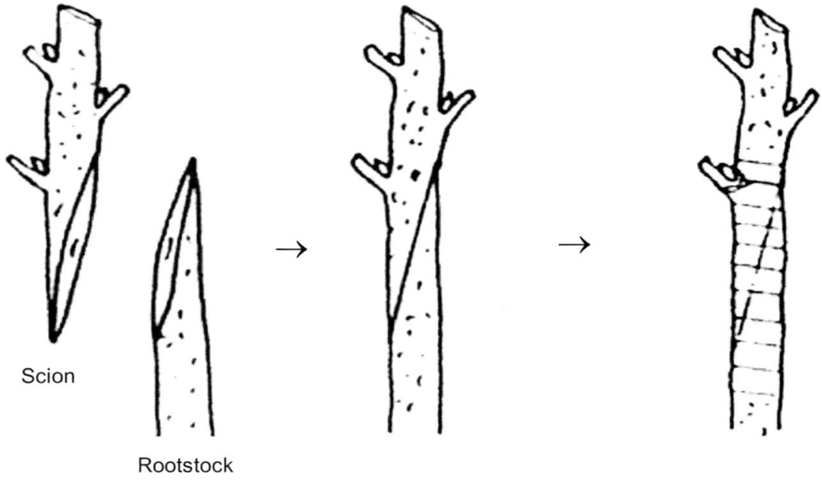

Fig. 19.3 Splice/Whip Grafting

19.5.5 Cleft grafting

i) Raise the stock plant prepared from cuttings in nursery pot. This method is used to graft cacti, particularly those having finger like stems.

ii) Select stock having a diameter of about 2.5 cm or more.

iii) A clean horizontal cut is made across the stock. Then, a cleft of about 3-6 cm is opened across the centre inside which the scion, tapered to a point from both side, is inserted.

iv) The stock may be tied with raffia to keep the scion secured. Scion and stock could be held together by passing a cactus thorn through both stock and scion at the middle of the union.

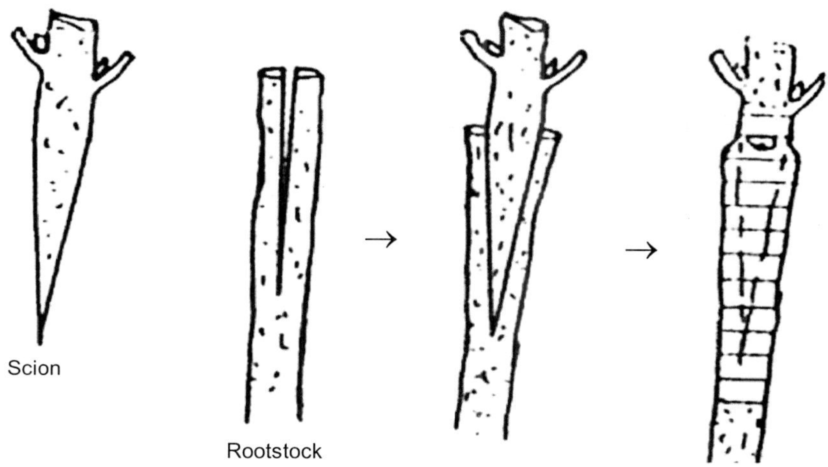

Fig. 19.4 Cleft Grafting

19.5.6 Other methods of grafting

a) Epicotyl or stone grafting

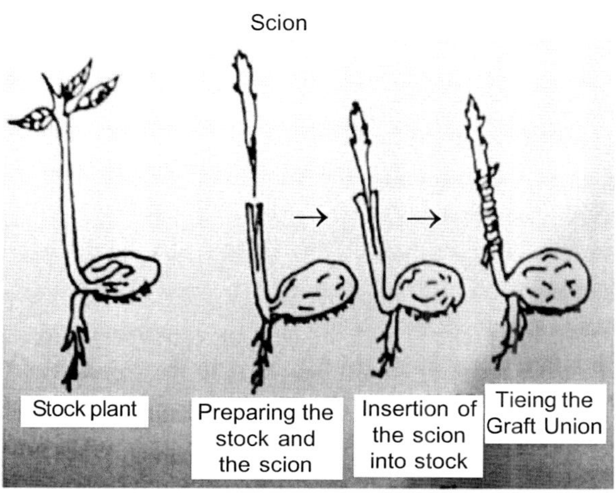

b) Tongue grafting

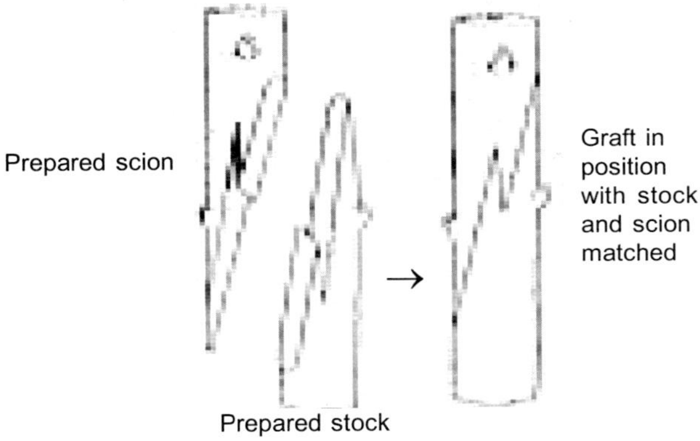

c) Saddle grafting

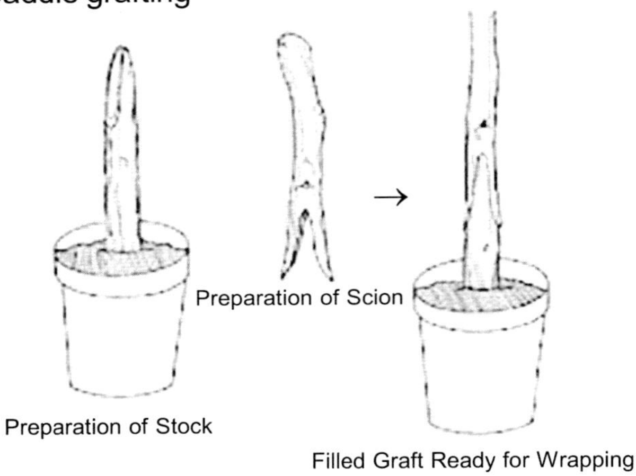

d) Bark Grafting

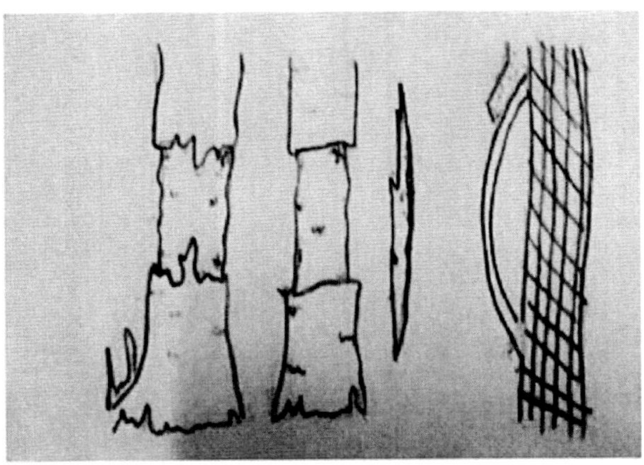

e) Bridge grafting

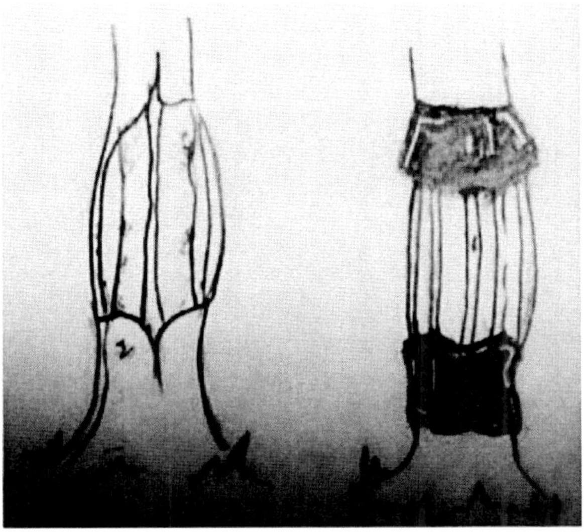

f) Top working

Important Notes

....

....

....

....

....

....

....

....

....

....

Lab Report

1. Propagate ornamental plants through different methods of grafting.

Name/Type of the plant	Method of grafting adopted	Number of grafts made	Date of grafting	Days taken in sprouting of scion	Number of grafts survived	Percentage of survival	Rate of survival after transplanting in field

Result:

Precautions:

2. Visit to various nurseries to learn about propagation through grafting in ornamental plants.

❑❑❑

LAB ACTIVITY-20

Propagation: Budding

20.1 Objective

To study propagation through budding.

20.2 Introduction

Budding is a type of grafting with the difference that instead of scion having multiple buds or scion nodes, a scion twig having a single bud is implanted in the stock.

20.3 Principle

Callus formation at the bud union results in the formation of cambial bridge between stock and scion and causes healing of the bud union, because of which they grow as one united plant.

20.4 Materials Required

Budding knife, secateur, tying material (polythene tape), petridish, scion bud, rootstock.

20.5 Types and Methods of Budding

20.5.1 Patch budding

Patch budding is generally used to propagate ornamental plants like hibiscus hybrids, standard rose cultivars and to propagate some flowering trees, which do not propagate by cutting or layering like *Gulmohar*.

i) One year old rootstock already raised in the nursery should be selected. A rectangular patch of bark is removed completely from the rootstock by two parallel cut at 3.5 cm apart and 2.5 cm long through the bark.

ii) Select scion bud free from disease from tha mother plant from the current season growth with dormant bud. A similar patch of bark of similar dimensions as on the rootstock and having a bud, is cut from the scion stick in the same manner.

iii) The bud is immediately placed on the rootstock which is already prepared and tied tightly with polythene tape leaving the bud open.

iv) After 4-6 weeks, when the bud is sprouted, the rootstock above the union is cut.

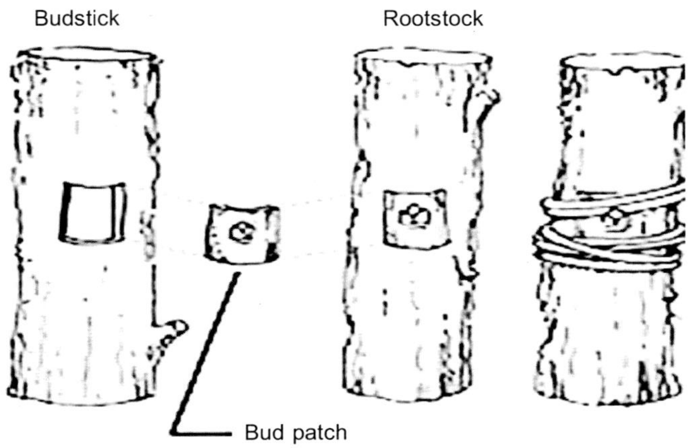

Fig: 20.1 Patch Budding

20.5.2 'T'- Budding

i) This technique is the modified form of patch budding. The rootstock on which the budding operation has to be performed, should be 10-20 mm in diameter or of pencil thickness. The budding operation should be done during the active growth stage of the stock plant, when the bark slips well.

ii) A 'T'-shape cut is made on the stock at 15-20 cm above the ground level by giving a vertical cut of 2.5 cm long on the stock followed by a right angled horizontal cut at the top with help of budding knife. Care should be taken so that the wood is not injured while making the cut.

iii) Select scion bud, free from disease, from the mother plant of the current season growth with a dormant bud. The shield shaped buds of 2.5 cm are taken by slicing 1.0 cm below and 1.0 cm above the leaf axis.

iv) Open the two flaps of the bark with the help of knife. The bud is then inserted gently into the 'T' cut on the stock plant and tied with the polythene tape, leaving the bud exposed.

v) After sprouting of the bud, the polythene tape is removed and the rootstock cut above the union. This technique is beneficial for species which are slow growing and where it takes a long time for scion wood of required maturity to develop.

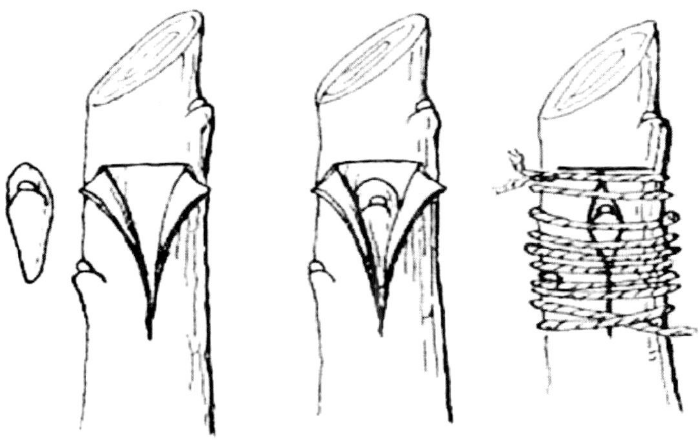

Fig. 20.2 T-Budding

20.5.3 Other methods of Budding

a) Inverted T budding

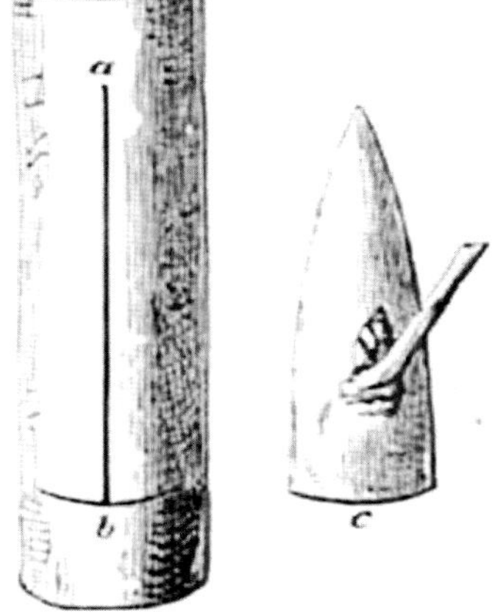

b) I budding

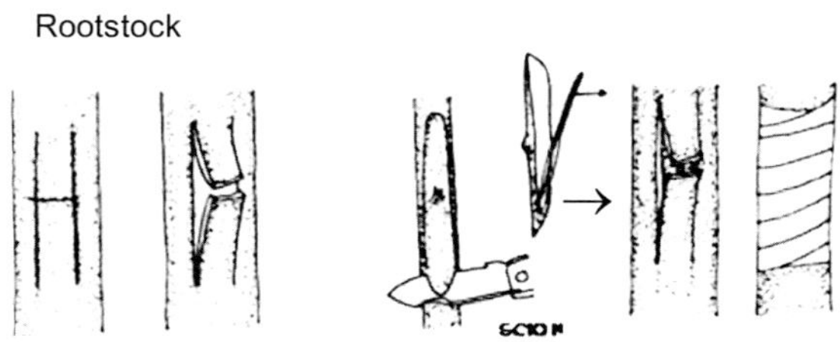

c) Forkert budding

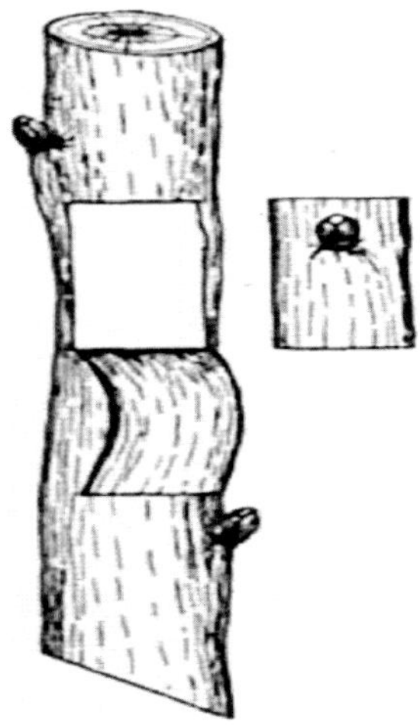

d) Modified forkert budding

e) Ring budding

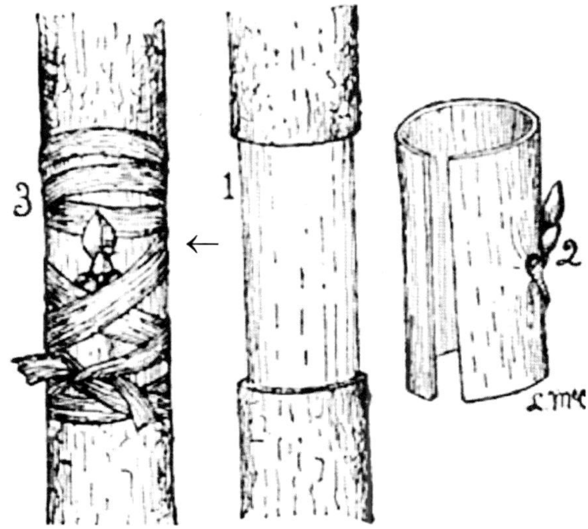

f) Flute budding

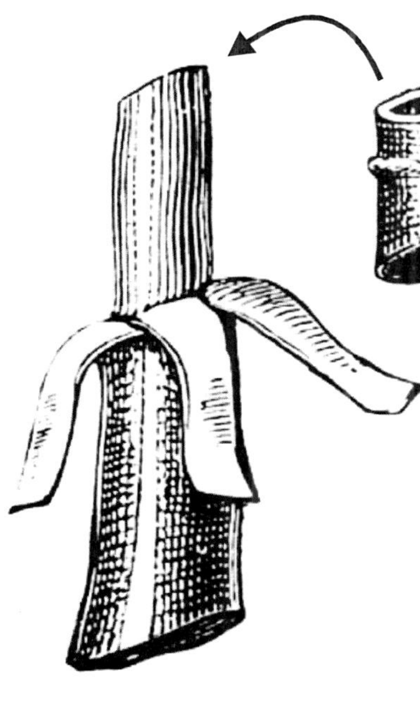

Important Notes

....

....

....

....

....

....

....

....

....

....

Lab Report

1. Propagate ornamental plants through different methods of budding.

Name/ Type of the plant	Method of budding adopted	Number of stocks budded	Date of budding	Days to bud sprouting	Number of bud survived	Percentage of survival	Rate of survival after transplantin g in field

Result:

Precautions:

2. Visit to various nurseries to learn propagation through budding of other ornamental plants.

❑❑❑

LAB ACTIVITY-21

Propagation: Specialized Structures

21.1 Objective

To study propagation through specialised structures.

21.2 Introduction

In some cases, modified plant parts which may be the stem, roots or leaves, usually specialized for food storage are used for propagation through separation. The plant showing these modifications constitute valuable and interesting flowering ornamental plants.

21.3 Bulbs

The term 'bulb' refers to a short, thickened, fleshy, vertical underground stem axis, bearing at its apex, a growing point or a flower primordium, enclosed by thick, fleshy scales. There are two types of bulbs: tunicate bulb and non-tunicate bulb.

21.3.1 Method of Propagation

i) Small bulbils are produced by the mother bulbs in the axil of leaves, which on development, are called as bulblets.

ii) These bulblets are detached from the mother bulb and planted in soil for further multiplication.

e.g. Tulip, Daffodils, Lily, Crinum, Narcissus, etc.

iii) In some plants, bulb cuttings can be used in which fully mature bulb is cut into small segments, containing a piece of basal plant and 3-4 scales.

iv) These segments are planted vertically in a suitable medium.

v) New bulblets will develop from these segments under favourable condition. e.g. Lycoris, Scilla, Narcissus, Haemanthus and Hymenocallis, etc.

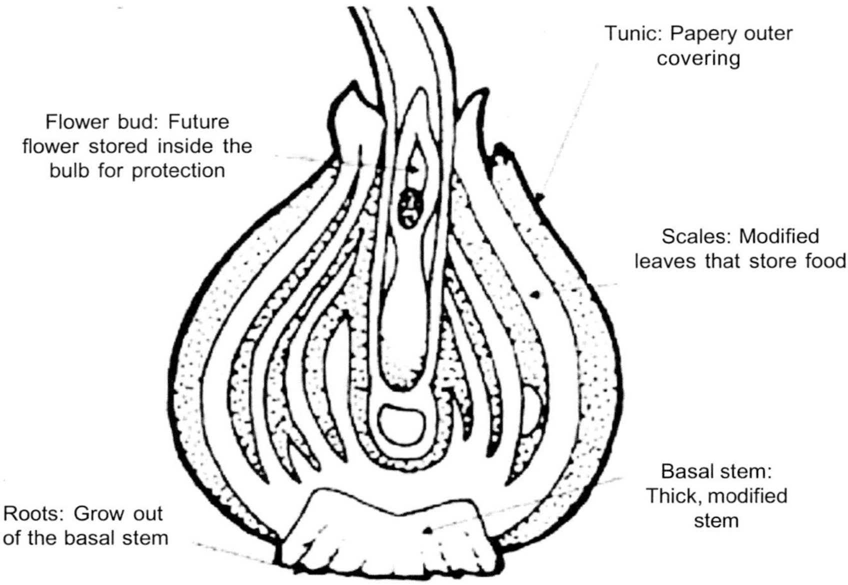

Fig. 21.1 Structure of a typical bulb and its parts

21.4 Corms

A corm is a short, much swollen horizental underground stem with one or several buds near the top, a tuft of leaves at the upper side and a ring of thick fibrous roots around the base.

21.4.1 Methods of propagation

Corms & Cormlets

i) After digging the plants, new corms and cormlets are separated and corms are sorted and graded according to size.

ii) The corms are then cured at 35°C for few hours and stored at 5°C and 70-80 per cent relative humidity in a well-ventilated room.

iii) These corms may be planted next year.

e.g. Gladiolus, Crocus, etc.

Fig. 21.2 Structure of a typical corm

21.5 Rhizome

Rhizomes are underground dorsiventral stems or branches growing horizontally under the surface of the soil. They are characterized by the presence of distinct nodes and internodes, scale leaves at the nodes, axillary and terminal buds and nodal roots.

21.5.1 Method of propagation

i) Rhizome is cut into sections. Each section should have at least one lateral bud or eye.

ii) These sections are planted in a suitable medium.

iii) Adventitious roots and new shoots develop from the nodes ultimately into a new plant.

Eg. Canna, Iris, Water lily and Water Hyacinth

Fig. 21.3 Structure of a typical rhizome

21.6 Tuber

Tuber is the swollen tip of lower branch which growes under the soil surface and is adapted for food storage and has axillary buds called eyes in the axils of scale leaves. The potato tuber also contains an apical (terminal) bud.

21.6.1 Method of Propagation

i) Every piece of tuber containing a bud is potentially capable of producing a new plant.

ii) Tuber is cut into sections. Each section must have at least one lateral bud or eye.

iii) These sections are planted in a suitable medium.

iv) Adventitious roots and new shoots develop from the nodes into a new plant.

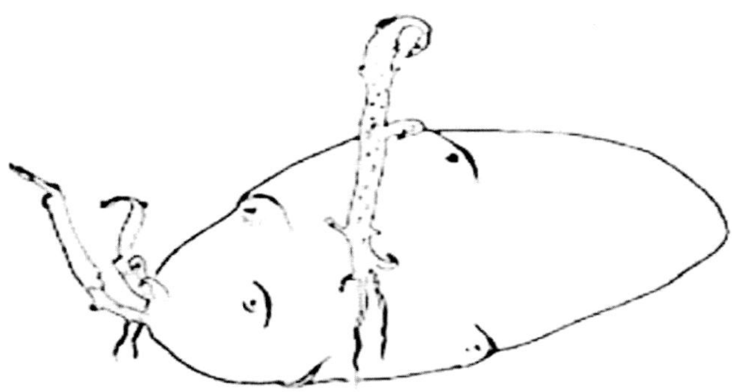

Fig. 21.4 Structure of a typical tuber

21.7 Tuberous Root

Tuberous roots are swollen roots and have abundant stores of reserve food which is used during active growth at the time of sowing.

21.7.1 Method of Propagation

i) Tuberous roots are detached from the mother plant and put into a suitable propagating media or deep into the soil.

ii) These roots produce shoots which develop into a new plant.

Fig. 21.5 Structure of tuberous root

21.8 Suckers

A sucker is an underground runner, which soon emerges to from a daughter plant, after striking roots.

21.8.1 Methods of propagation

i) Suckers are separated from the mother plant and planted either in the nursery or directly in the field for rooting. e.g. Pineapple, Chrysanthemum.

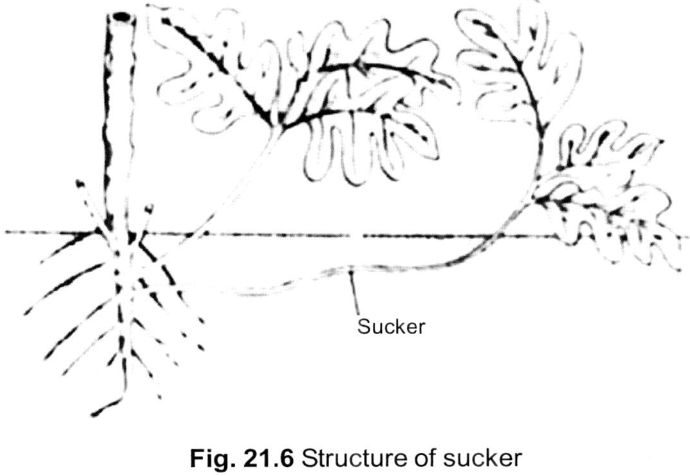

Fig. 21.6 Structure of sucker

21.9 Runners

A runner is a long, slender stem which grow from the axil of a leaf at the crown of a plant and trails along the ground and forms a new plant at one of the nodes.

21.9.1 Methods of propagation

i) Runners are produced from the leaf axil at the crown of a plant and prostate horizontally along the ground.

ii) The roots appear at one of the nodes having contact with soil.

iii) After root formation in the new plants, the contact with the mother plant is automatically detached and the new plants can be separated and planted in the field or nursery. e.g. Doob grass (*Cynodon dactylon*), fern and spider plant which is commercially propagated through runner.

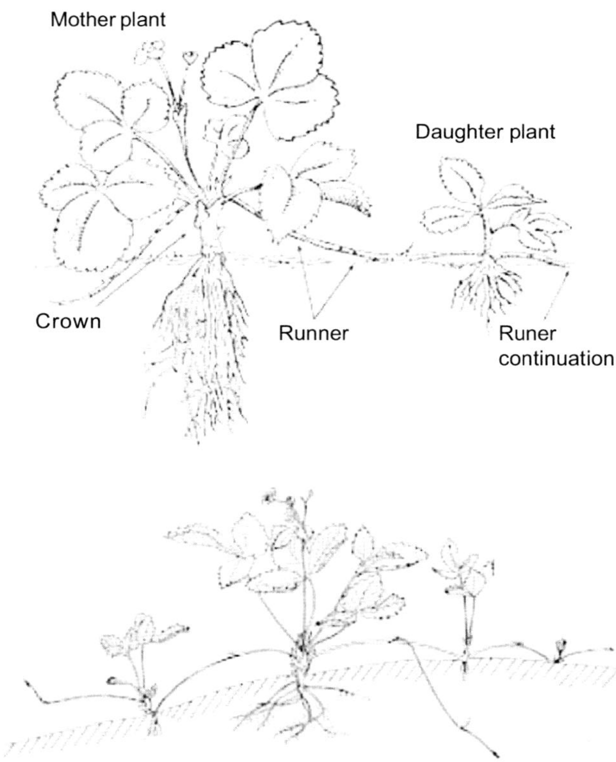

Fig. 21.7 Structure of runner

Important Notes

....

....

....

....

....

....

....

....

....

....

Lab Report

1. Propagate ornamental plants through different modified structures.

Name/ Type of the plant	Modified structures	Date of planting	Days to bud sprouting	Number of plant survived	Percentage of survival

Result:

Precautions:

2. Visit to various nurseries to learn about propagation through special structures of ornamental plants.

❑❑❑

LAB ACTIVITY-22

Micropropagation

22.1 Objective

To study different stages in micropropagation.

22.2 Introduction

Micro propagation or tissue culture is basically multiplication/ propagation of plants from a small plant organ, tissue or cells in test tubes or an artificial media under controlled temperature and light conditions in a laboratory under aseptic conditions. It is, thus, also called *in-vitro* culture. There are basically three steps in the process of micropropagation before the plant can be transferred to the pot or field under an open environment:

a) Sterilization of explants and its establishment

b) Proliferation or differentiation of explants

c) Hardening of micropropagated plants

22.3 Ornamental plants suitable for micropropagation

Cordyline, Dracaena, Alstroemeria, Amaryllis, Hippeastrum, Narcissus, Nerine, Clivia, Chrysanthemum, Gerbera, Begonia, Ananas, Billbergia, Weigela, Dianthus, Euphorbia, Pelargonium, Gloxinia, Saintpaulia, Freesia, Gladiolus, Iris, Sparaxis, Schizostylis, Aloe, Hemerocallis, Hyacinthus, Lilium, Ornithogalum, Scilla, Orchid, Cyclamen, Phlox, Antirrhinum, Petunia etc.

22.4 Materials Required

1. Shoot tip of gerbera plant
2. $HgCl_2$ solution (1%)- for sterilizing explants
3. MS basal medium (1000 ml)
4. Benzyl aminopurine (1mM stock)

5. NAA (1 mM stock)
6. Glasswares and others- Beakers, Measuring cylinders, Conical flasks Forceps, Blade Holder, Sterilzed blades, Micropipettes, cork borers, petridishes.
7. Cotton plugs
8. Sucrose
9. Agar Agar 10 g/l (1%)
10. Laminar flow air cabinet

22.5 Preparation of MS medium

- MS Major (20X) 50 ml
- MS Minor (200X) 5 ml
- MS Vitamin (200X) 5 ml
- Iron (200X) 5 ml
- Sucrose 30 gm (3%)

→ Add BAP at this stage (1mM stock)

→ Make final volume to 1000 ml by double distilled water

→ Set pH at 5.8

→ Add agar agar 8 gm/L (0.8%), melt the agar agar in microwave oven

→ Sterilize the media at 15 psi/121^0 C for 15 minutes

→ After autoclaving, gently swirl the medium to mix the agar. When the agar is completely dissolved and mixed, the medium should appear clear and not turbid.

→ Add filter sterilized NAA, once the temperature of the medium cools down to 60^0 C.

22.6 Procedure

i) Initiation Stage

In this step, the excised tissue or the explants is obtained. The main criterion in this step is to obtain sterilized, microbial infestation free explants. Gerbera plants should be separated into divisions and then leaves are stripped off completely from each division reducing it to a bud piece measuring only 0.5-1.0 cm in length. This piece is composed of the terminal bud and a portion of the subjacent stem. After this, disinfect, this piece by immersing in $HgCl_2$ solution (1%) for some time (10 sec). The pieces are then rinsed thrice with autoclaved water and cut further till shoot tip explants measuring 2-3 mm is obtained. This requires a dissecting microscope.

ii) Multiplication Stage

In this step, the actual propagule multiplication is obtained. The explant is placed in MS medium for callus production at 1% agar base. The pH of medium should be 5.8 and the culture was kept in normal day light at 25±5°C. Callus can be sub-cultured again and again till the required number of embryos, shoots, organs are obtained. All operation should be performed in laminar air flow cabinet.

iii) Acclimatization Stage

A growing, rooted shoot can be removed from tissue culture planted in a pot and kept in a shaded location for acclimatization before planting in open conditions. When this is done, the humidity must be gradually reduced over time because tissue-cultured plants are extremely susceptible to wilting. The clonally multiplied plants are then transferred from media to soil.

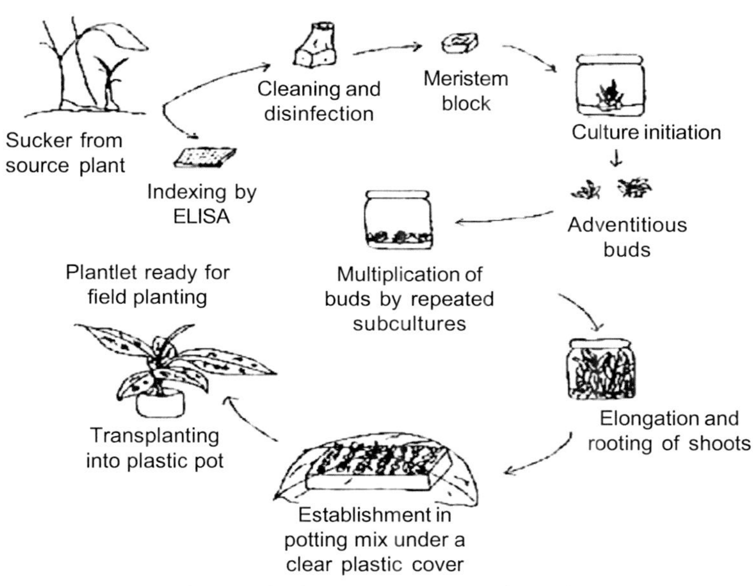

Fig. 24.1 Stages in the micropropagation of gerbera

Important Notes

....

....

....

....

....

....

....

....

....

....

Lab Report

1. Prepare 500 ml nutrient stock solution of MS media for micro-propagation of Gerbera and Orchid.
2. Discuss in detail the various stages of micropropagation of ornamental plants.
3. What are the advantages and limitations of micropropagation technique?

❑❑❑

LAB ACTIVITY-23

Micropropagation: Media

23.1 Objective

Preparation of stock solutions of Murashige & Skoog (MS) basal medium and plant growth regulator stocks for micropropagation.

23.2 Introduction

The basal medium for tissue culture was formulated by Murashige & Skoog in 1962 so that all the elements needed for growth and development of plants could be made available artificially under micropropagation systems. The medium used for tissue culture consists of 95% water, macro- and micronutrients, vitamins, amino acids, sugars. The nutrients in the media are used by the plant cells as building blocks for the synthesis of organic molecules or for catalysing enzymatic reactions. The macronutrients *viz;* (N, P, K, Ca, Mg etc) are required in millimolar (mM) quantities while micronutrients *viz;* (B, Mn, Zn, Fe, etc.) are needed in much lower (micromolar, µM) concentrations. Vitamins are organic substances that are part of enzymes or cofactors for essential metabolic functions. Sugar is essential for *in-vitro* growth and development, as most plant cultures are unable to photosynthesize effectively in the vital establishment phase for a variety of reasons. Murashige & Skoog medium (MS) is the most suitable and commonly used basic tissue culture medium for plant regeneration.

Plant growth regulators (PGRs) *viz;* auxin, cytokinins, gibberellins, etc. at a very low concentration (0.1 to 100 µM) regulate the initiation and development of shoots and roots on explants on semisolid or in liquid medium cultures. The relative auxin and cytokinin ratio in culture media determines the morphogenesis in cultured tissues.

23.3 Materials Required

- Amber bottles
- Plastic beakers (100 ml, 500 ml and 1000 ml)

- Measuring cylinders (500 ml)
- Glass beakers (50 ml)
- Autoclaved eppendorf tubes (2 ml)
- Eppendorf stand
- Benzyl-aminopurine
- Naphthalene acetic acid

23.4 MS Nutrient Stock Solutions

Nutrient salts and vitamins are prepared as stock solutions (20X or 200 X concentrations of that required in the medium), as specified. The stocks are stored at 4^0 C. The desired amount of concentrated stocks is mixed to prepare 1 litre of medium.

23.4.1 Stock solution of macronutrients

MS major salts	mg/1 L medium	500 ml stock (20X)
1. NH_4NO_3	1650 mg	16.5 gm
2. KNO_3	1900 mg	19 gm
3. $Cacl_2.2H_2O$	440 mg	4.4 gm
4. $MgSO_4.7H_2O$	370 mg	3.7 gm
5. KH_2PO_4	170 mg	1.7 gm

23.4.2 Stock solution of micronutrients

MS minor salts	mg/1 L medium	500 ml stock (200X)
1. H_3BO_3	6.2 mg	620 mg
2. $MnSO_4.4H_2O$	22.3 mg	2230 mg
3. $ZnSO_{4.}4H_2O$	8.6 mg	860 mg
4. KI	0.83 mg	83 mg
5. $Na_2MoO_{4.}2H_2O$	0.25 mg	25 mg
6. $CoCl_{2.}6H_2O$	0.025 mg	2.5 mg
7. $CuSO_{4.}5H_2O$	0.025 mg	2.5 mg

23.4.3 Stock solution of vitamins

MS Vitamins	mg/1 L medium	500 ml stock (200X)
1. Thiamine (HCl)	0.1 mg	10 mg
2. Niacine	0.5 mg	50 mg
3. Glycine	2.0 mg	200 mg
4. Pyrodoxine (HCl)	0.5 mg	50 mg

23.4.4 Iron Stock Soloution (200x) 500ml

1. Dissolve 3.725 gm of Na_2EDTA (Ethylene diaminetetra acetic acid, disodium salt) in 250 ml dH_2O.
2. Dissolve 2.785gm of $FeSO_4.7H_2O$ in 250 ml dH_2O.
3. Boil Na_2EDTA solution and add to it, $FeSO_4$ solution gently by stirring.

23.4.5 Plant Growth Regulator Stock

1. The heat-labile plant growth regulators are filtered through a bacteria-proof membrane (0.22 μm) filter and added to the autoclaved medium, once cooled below 60°C.
2. The stocks of plant growth regulators are prepared as mentioned below:

Plant Growth Regulator	Nature	Mol. Wt.	Stock (1 mM)	Soluble in
Benzyl aminopurine	Autoclavable	225.2	mg/ ml	1N NaOH
Naphtalene acetic acid	Heat labile	186.2	mg/ ml	Ethanol

The desired amount of plant growth regulators is dissolved as above and the volume is made up to one litre with double distilled water.

Important Notes

....

....

....

....

....

....

....

....

....

....

Lab Report

1. Prepare 500 ml of stock solution of macronutrient for MS nutrient media.
2. Prepare 500 ml of stock solution of micronutrient for MS nutrient solution.
3. Prepare 500 ml of stock solution of vitamins for MS nutrient solution.
4. Prepare 500 ml iron stock solution for MS nutrient solution.

❑❑❑

LAB ACTIVITY-24

Micropropagation: Sterilization

22.1 Objective

Sterilization of culture media.

22.2 Principle

Under tissue culture systems, microbes present in the environment, media, equipments, plant part used for tissue culture, technician in itself may cause infection in the culture system. This infection can be due to:

1. Air-containing a large quantity of suspended microorganisms in the form of fungal and bacterial spores.
2. Plant tissue-pathogens on its surface.
3. Human body, skin, human breath, etc. carries several micro-organisms.

Thus, before undertaking tissue culture, all culture vessels, media and instruments used in handling tissues as well as the explants must be sterilized. Subsequently, all the operations must be carried out in laminar air-flow, a sterile cabinet to prevent infection in the culture.

There are different methods of sterilization to eliminate sources of infection:

1. **Autoclave:** Preparation of sterile media, culture vessels and instruments
2. **Filtration:** Preparation of sterile plant growth regulators stocks
3. **Laminar Air Flow**: Aseptic working condition
4. **Chemicals:** Explants (isolated tissues) are sterilized using chemical sterilants, e.g. $HgCl_2$ and NaOCl.

22.3 Methods of sterilization

22.3.1 Autoclaving (Steam or Wet sterilization)

It this method super heated steam is used under pressure as in a domestic pressure cooker. Instruments/ nutrient media/glassware are sterilized in an autoclave at a temperature of 115- 135^{0}C. The standard condition for autoclaving has a temperature of 121^{0}C for 15-20 minutes at 15 psi. The time taken for liquids to reach this temperature depends on their volume or thickness of the vessel.

22.3.2 Filtration

Some growth regulators like amino acids and vitamins are heat labile and get destroyed on autoclaving with the rest of the nutrient medium. Therefore, they are filtered through a sieve or a filtration assembly using micro filter membranes of 0.22 ìm to 0.45ìm size.

22.3.3 Irradiation

UV lights may be used to kill organisms in rooms or areas of work benches, in which manipulation of cultures is carried out. A UV light is provided in the laminar air flow cabinet which may be switched on for required duration before culturing or sterilisation of all glassware to be used during the process of tissue culture.

22.3.4 Laminar Airflow Cabinet

This is the primary equipment used for creating an aseptic environment for performing tissue culture. This cabinet is used for creating horizontal air-flow from the back to the front. Air is drawn in electric fans and passed through the coarse filter and then through the fine bacterial filter HEPA or High Efficiency Particulate Air Filter. The air filters should be cleaned and changed periodically and care taken not to disturb this flow too much by vigorous movements. Before commencing any experiment, it is desirable to clean the working surface with 70% alcohol and surface sterilisation of the chamber and glassware, etc. by UV rays.

22.4 Precautions

i) Excessive autoclaving should be avoided, as it will degrade sucrose and agar under prolonged heating.

ii) At the bottom of the autoclave required level of water should be ensured.

iii) While autoclaving bottles should not be tightly screwed and their tops should be loose.

iv) Air filter of the laminar air flow should be changed periodically.

Important Notes

....

....

....

....

....

....

....

....

....

....

Lab Report

1. Enlist various techniques of sterilization and compare them with each other.
2. Why sterilization is an essential process in micropropagation?

❑❑❑

Section D:

NURSERY MANAGEMENT

LAB ACTIVITY-25

Nursery Management: Records

25.1 Objective

To study preparation and maintenance of nursery records.

25.2 Introduction

Some records are essential for nurserymen to plan the nursery for remunerative returns and establish itself as a reputed enterprise. A nursery planner should know how long it takes to lift saplings or how much seed is required, or how much cuttings he can accommodate in a glasshouse or how much scion wood is required for grafting a particular plot of nursery. There must be specific register for specific selected activities to keep day-to-day or pedigree or operation records in nursery. These records are required by law to satisfy inspecting authorities, tax calculation, detect or discourage theft in case of big nurseries. The important aspects for which maintenance of record is necessary are as under:

25.3 Materials Required

Registers, chronological operation record and nursery map

25.4 Procedure

25.4.1 Progeny orchard record

The exact map of progeny orchard is drawn in a register, which depicts the date of plantation, source of mother orchard plants, layout record of different fruit varieties. The addition or deletion of any variety needs to be recorded chronologically. The quantity of scion wood taken from individual mother plant should also be recorded, so as to quantify the volume of cuttings per plant and total strength of mother plants required to be maintained to cater to the demand/need of particular customers.

25.4.2 Nursery layout record

The layout plan of nursery plots crop wise, and within crop variety wise, mentioning direction of plots should be maintained. The plots should also be labelled with tags or field plates, if there is no risk of theft. This helps in ensuring the proper record along with date of budding/ grafting, days taken to sprout, etc.

25.4.3 Cultural operations record

The record of different operations, such as stratification of seeds, date of sowing, date of germination, farm operation such as record of spray dates, date of budding / grafting , fertilizer application and dose applied should be maintained. Any other foliar spray including insecticides, fungicides, growth regulators and nutrient sprays etc. must be recorded.

25.4.4 Disposal register

The record of saleable plants left after thorough inspection is maintained in this register. The record is maintained crop wise, variety wise, which will tell us the expected out come from the nursery and help in accounting purposes.

25.4.5 Advisory/visitor register

The suggestions of experts invited to address specific problem should be recorded in this register, with his own hand. The record of visitors should be maintained with specific remarks and feedback from the field. Some of the valuable remarks of experts and experienced nurserymen can be put in practice.

25.5 Precautions

1. All registers should be issued through Inventory Register, so that record of number of registers maintained is known.
2. The specific information should be recorded.
3. Nurserymen should not be bias in recording specific problems.

Important Notes

....

....

....

....

....

....

....

....

....

....

Lab Report

1. Why is it essential to maintain and prepare nursery records?
2. Enlist and discuss the special nursery activities for maintaining nursery record register.

❑❑❑

LAB ACTIVITY-26

Preparation of Nursery Plants

26.1 Objective

To study uprooting/digging, labelling and packing of nursery plants.

26.2 Introduction

In a commercial nursery for successful marketing of the nursery plants, it is essential to properly uproot the plants without damage, label the plants having all essential information and then proper packaging for long distance and safe transportation of the nursery plants.

26.3 Materials Required

Digging/uprooting tools, labels, sphagnum moss, markers, wrapping material (Hessian cloth).

26.4 Procedure

26.4.1 Uprooting/digging of nursery

i) To avoid the damage to the roots, it is advisable to irrigate nursery, 3- 4 days before the actual date of lifting the plants. The lifting of (evergreen spp.) saplings should however be avoided, in case if there is heavy rain in the rainy season because earth ball does not form properly if soil is too wet.

ii) To achieve high rate of yield survival of evergreen tropical or subtropical ornamental plants like Pine, Juniper, Acacia, etc. these should be uprooted with a ball of earth.

iii) In case of deciduous plants like plumeria, Delonix, Ceiba, Azelia, Lagerstromia, Bauhinia, Ceasalpinia, etc. can be lifted bare rooted.

26.4.2 Inspection of nursery plants

i) The uprooted nursery plants should be inspected by the team of experts for thorough check up for parameters like infestation of diseases, attack of insects and healthy root system. The unhealthy saplings should be discarded before packing and storage of seedlings.

26.4.3 Labelling of nursery plants

i) After thorough inspection, the saplings should be labelled crop wise and variety wise with the help of zinc labels, plastic labels or wooden labels for proper identification and labelled sale of nursery plants.

26.4.4 Packing of nursery plants

i) After uprooting and labelling, the saplings should be properly packed. The bare rooted nursery plants of deciduous species should be placed with moist sphagnum moss and wrapped in hessian cloth to avoid drying of roots.

ii) The saplings should be wrapped with moist grass or rice straw before putting in polyethylene bags and then kept in baskets.

26.4.5 Packing materials

i) The different packing materials used for packing of nursery plants are hessian cloth, sacking cloth, paddy straw, dried grasses and plastics, etc.

ii) The hessian cloth is derived from the best jute, whereas sacking cloth is made from raw grade jute fibre.

iii) Different plastic material includes low density polyethylene (LDPE), high density polythene (HDPE), polypropylene (PP) and nylon, etc.

26.5 Precautions

i) While uprooting nursery plants, damage to root system should be avoided.

ii) Plants offered for sale should be uniform and true to type.

iii) No negligence in inspection of nursery plants.

iv) The packing of nursery plants should be done carefully to avoid drying of root system.

Important Notes

....

....

....

....

....

....

....

....

....

....

Lab Report

1. Discuss and write about the uprooting and digging of different nursery plants. What precautions should be kept in mind while uprooting?
2. What essential information should be written in a properly labelled nursery plants?
3. Enlist different types of packaging materials used for packaging of nursery plants for long distance transportation.

❏❏❏

Section E:

HI-TECH NURSERY

LAB ACTIVITY-27

Raising Nursery Through Hi-Tech Methods in Protrays

27.1 Objective

To study about nursery raising technique in protrays.

27.2 Introduction

Quality planting material is the primary requirement for any commercial nursery to be successful since it gives the required quick start to the crop resulting in optimum growth ensuring efficient utilisation of the natural resources like water, sunlight, etc. and the inherent potential of the plant.

Conventionally, seeds were sown in raised nursery beds in open fields, either in lines or as broadcast. Survival of these plants was poor since they were infected with soil borne pathogens resulting in damping off leading to high mortality. Uniform distribution of the seed, moisture, nutrients, etc. to all the seeds in the nursery beds was not possible and seedlings were also lost due to root damage upon being pulled out from the seedling beds prior to transplanting.

With the advent of hybrid seeds, where the cost of seeds was high, hi-tech methods for raising seedlings were developed, where seeds are sown individually in specially designed trays, in soilless, artificial and sterile media (cocopeat, vermiculite, etc.) and fed with controlled quantity of moisture and liquid nutrients at regular intervals until they are ready for transplanting. These are placed in protected enclosures like shadehouses, polyhouses or polytunnels, etc., to protect them from inclement weather. An added benefit is that nursery can be developed in a small area with low fertility lands even in highly dense urban cities through the technical skill of raising nursery in these plastic portable propagation trays (protrays).

27.3 Materials required

i) **Seedling trays or protrays:** Re-usable polypropylene trays having 98, 102 or 104 cells having a cavity depth of 4 to 5 cm with a hole at the base are commonly used. The trays need to be washed and disinfected with fungicide before use.

Fig. 27.1 Nursery Protrays

ii) **Media for sowing seed**: Well decomposed sterile media are successfully used since they prevent incidence of pathogenic infections commonly observed in soil, FYM or other organic manure. Cocopeat is the most common media used in commercial nurseries. Vermicompost may also be used in place of cocopeat. By using propagating media, other than soil, in nursery protrays we can transport them easily over long distances since the media are light and do not have any phytosanitary obligations.

Fig. 27.2 Filling protrays with propagating media

iii) **Protected structures**: Low cost polyhouses and nethouses constructed on bamboo or metal frames are generally used for raising seedlings. Polytunnels are also successfully used to protect from rainfall. The seedling trays are placed on raised metal racks or cemented platforms in the protected structures.

Fig. 27.3 Nursery raising seedlings in protrays on raised platform under protected structures.

iv) **Nutrient formulations**: Water soluble fertilizers (containing NPK and trace elements).

27.4 Stages for raising nursery in protrays

i) Large sized seeds, such as tomato, brinjal, cucurbits, cole crops, etc. May be sown individually in each cavity of the protray.

ii) Smaller sized seeds, generally in the ornamental plants, are sown in small beds filled with cocopeat and after germination one seedling each is then planted in one cavity of the protray.

Fig. 27.4 Seed sowing in individual cells of protrays

Fig. 27.5 Fully grown seedlings ready for transplanting

iii) Irrigation: Watering of the seedlings may be done with a rose can. In some nurseries, water along with the nutrient solution is filled in the cavities on cemented platforms on which the trays are placed so that it is applied from the base of the trays through the holes in each cavity of the tray.

iv) Nutrition: 3g/l water soluble fertilizers containing NPK and trace elements is sprayed on the seedlings or may be applied from the base alongwith the irrigation water.

v) Seedlings may be sprayed with copper oxychloride (3g/l) and carbendazim (1g/l) to protect from damping off.

vi) Seedlings may be transplanted in the main field 3-6 weeks after sowing.

27.5 Precautions

If seedlings have been raised under a polyhouse, then watering should be withheld and shade should be reduced for 1-2 days before transplanting to improve the establishment of the seedlings in the field.

27.6 Advantages of Hi-tech nursery raising (in protrays)

- Seed germination is improved and mortality due to pathogens is reduced
- Transplanting shock is negligible since roots of seedlings are not disturbed
- Ease in handling and transport over large distances since media used is light

- Uniform growth in nursery which ensures better establishment and performance of seedlings on field
- Facilitates uniform maturity of the crop.
- Vertical spaces can be effectively utilised through multi–tier nursery raising.
- Nursery can be established, even if there is less land available.

Important Notes

....

....

....

....

....

....

....

....

....

....

Lab Report

1. Raise the nursery of any five vegetables /winter annuals in portrays and note down the following observations:

Name of the plant	No. of portrays used	Propagating media	Time taken to germination (days)	Germination percentage
1.				
2				
3.				

2. Compare nursery raising in soil and protrays and write down its advantages and disadvantages on the basis of following observations:

Name of the plant	Area		Propagating media		Quantity of seeds (g)		Time taken to germination (days)		Rate of mortality		Germination percentage	
	Soil	Protray	Soil	Protrays	Soil	Protrays	Soil	Protrays	Soil	Protrays	Soil	Protrays

❑❑❑